ENCYCLOPAEDIA OF EMINENT THINKERS

VOLUME-XXIII: **PANDIT DEENDAYAL UPADHYAYA**

Volumes by the same author

The Political Thought of ***Veer Savarkar***
The Political Thought of ***M.A. Jinnah***
The Political Thought of ***Mohammad Iqbal***
The Political Thought of ***K.B. Hedgewar***
The Political Thought of ***M.S. Golwalkar***
The Political Thought of ***Lokmanya Bal Gangadhar Tilak***
The Political Thought of ***Pandit Deendayal Upadhyaya***
The Political Thought of ***Gopal Krishna Gokhale***
The Political Thought of ***Maulana Abul Kalam Azad***
The Political Thought of ***Sir Syed Ahmed Khan***

About the Author

Dr. Jai Narain Sharma (*b.* 1951) is Professor and Chairman of the Department of Gandhian Studies, Panjab University, Chandigarh. He is also Hon. Director of Gandhi Bhawan; member of Board of Studies, Nagpur University, Nagpur and Mahatma Gandhi Kashi Vidyapith, Varanasi; member of Research Degree Committee of the Department of Political Science, H.P. University, Shimla: General Secretary of Indian Soviety of Gandhian Studies; and member on the Presidium of the Alliance for Sarvodaya. He regularly writes for leading newspapers, and has published more than hundred research papers in professional journals of repute. Dr. Sharma has many books to his credit including *"Gandhi's View of Political Power", "Economics of Defence: A Study of SAARC Countries", "Economic Thought of Mahatma Gandhi", "Human Resource Management", "Alternative Economics: Economics of Mahatma Gandhi and Globalisation", "Power, Politics and Corruption: A Gandhian Solution"* and *"Research Methodology: The Discipline and its Dimensions.*

ENCYCLOPAEDIA OF EMINENT THINKERS

VOLUME-TWENTY THREE

THE POLITICAL THOUGHT OF PANDIT DEENDAYAL UPADHYAYA

Dr. Jai Narain Sharma
Professor and Chairman
Department of Gandhian Studies
Panjab University
Chandigarh

CONCEPT PUBLISHING COMPANY, NEW DELHI - 110 059

Cataloging in Publication Data—DK
Courtesy: D.K. Agencies (P) Ltd. docinfo@dkagencies.com

Encyclopaedia of eminent thinkers.
p. cm. — (Gandhian studies and peace research series ; 11)
Vols. 11- lack series statement.
In Indian context.
Includes bibliographical references.
Includes indexes.
Contents: v. 23. The political thought of Pandit Deendayal Upadhyaya / Jai Narain Sharma.
ISBN 13: 9788180695834
ISBN 10: 8180695832

1. Statesmen--India. 2. Political science—India. 3. India—Politics and government. I. Sharma, Jai Narain, 1951- II. Pasricha, ashu, 1967- III. Series: Gandhian studies and peace research series ; 11.

DDC 954.035 22

ISBN -13: 978-81-7022-684-0 (Series)
ISBN -10: 81-7022-684-8 (Series)
ISBN -13: 978-81-8069-583-4 (Vol. XXIII)
ISBN -10: 81-8069-583-2 (Vol. XXIII)

First Published 2009

Published and Printed by
Ashok Kumar Mittal
Concept Publishing Company
A/15-16, Commercial Block, Mohan Garden
New Delhi-110059 (India).

Phones: 25351460, 25351794
Fax: 091-11-25357103
E-mail: publishing@conceptpub.com

DEDICATED
TO
THE SACRED MEMORY
OF MY
ELDER BROTHER
(Late) DR. YOGESHWAR PRASHAD SHARMA

PREFACE

No single rule can be laid down as to the proper time for publicizing the personal life and thoughts of great men who made history. The time for exposition of personal life may or may not be proper for publication of thoughts.

In case of great men it appears that their contemporaries are not able to properly assess their work. The contemporaries face a difficulty: the problems of the day, the different attitudes adopted by different people, and the consequent prejudices. Just as people with normal eyesight, when caught in a dust storm with dust in their eyes, cannot see clearly things right before them; in the same way contemporary people, caught in the storms of events, are not able to properly assess the lives and work of great men. Real appreciation becomes possible only when the storm is over and vision is clear. This evaluating great man takes time—may be decades, on even centuries!

Such is this strange process. The people who crucified Jesus Christ had to change their assessment of him after 330 years. He was not only admitted to have been a great man but his gospel was accepted by the Roman Rulers. After Waterloo was lost, Napoleon's estimate by the entire French nation was very low. But after some decades the entire France realised that he was a very great man. His remains were very respectfully brought from St. Helina and statutes were erected in his memory.

Many such examples show that neither contemporary publicity nor popularity is a definite criterion of anybody's greatness. His greatness depends on how long a shadow his work casts on the future. Therefore, the contemporary assessment of any great or stormy personality cannot be accepted as standard.

In short, the greatness of a man cannot be assessed by contemporary evaluation, but can be best judged over a relatively long period of time.

Pandit Deendayal Upadhyaya was a prominent leader of a growing political party in post-independence India and also its chief organiser. Naturally, it was imperative for him to attend to the day-to-day problems of the country, governmental policies, elections, agitations, calamities, party propaganda—problems which political workers cannot escape. Yet it was a fortunate coincidence that Deendayal entered the field of politics after imbibing a certain view of life and training in value-based living. In fact, he accepted political party-work with a definite mission in his mind—viz. to project genuine nationalistic thought in the political sphere. As a result, he was not engulfed in the immediate and the expedient, nor was his study of problems restricted to the limited aim of the attainment of political power. He never accepted short-sighted compromises, nor did he allow himself to be carried away by the pressure of passing events and circumstances. In spite of being a political leader, his approach was that of a nation-builder. He visualized the activity of a political party only as a means to nation-building end. Consequently, his thinking on national issues touches wider horizons and is basic in character. He gave a jolt to many current ideas and nations, and through his writings he expounded his views on the ethos of our national life.

Some, it has been said, are born great, some achieve greatness, and some have greatness thrust upon them. Pandit Deendayal Upadhyaya belonged to the second category. Starting with the advantages of neither birth, wealth nor rank, yet he rose to the top rank of Indian Politics. Many important leaders fade away after death. Deendayal belonged to the class of the truly great who rise higher after their death.

After Panditji's death, it has been the desire of many that there should be research on his thought. However, it must be admitted that the available literature is very scanty.

When we speak of Deendayal's thoughts, his analysis, his inferences, there is no restrictive specific or distinctive connotation. It is nearlly a very difficult taste, in fact impossible to sparate his thought from his actions. Our national tradition speaks through them. Thinkers and philosophers like Deendayal, through their extraordinary genius, give only a new expression, in the light of the modern context, to those ideals and abiding philosophy which flowered in this soil for thousands of years and whose continuity thrived against all odds. They are modern exponents of our eternal national philosophy. The basic principles they propagate are not new. They are motivated by the sincere urge to remove the self-oblivion of their people and to awaken its consciousness and urge to act.

The present work is an humble attempt to outline the political ideas of this multi-splendourous personality. I hope the book will provide a glimpse – though not a full effulgent view of the Himalayan height of the personality of Pandit Deendayal Upadhyaya.

My special thanks are due to Professor S.L. Malhotra, Professor R.N. Pal, Professor N. Radhakrishnan, Dr. K.S. Bharathi, Dr. R.P. Divedi, Dr. A.D. Mishra, Professor B.R. Duggar, Dr. K.C. Agnihotri, Professor Raj Bir Singh Yadav, Professor M.L. Sharma, Dr. Meena Dutta, Dr. Ashu Pasricha and Dr. Rashmi Sharma. Besides, I offer an all embracing salute to the galaxy of the scholars whose works I have consulted.

I am also grateful to Shri Ashok Kumar Mittal, my publisher for his consistent zeal in the printing and publication of this volume.

Chandigarh **JAI NARAIN SHARMA**

Encyclopaedia of Eminent Thinkers Series

Vol. I. The Political Thought of Mahatma Gandhi/ *K.S. Bharti*
Vol. II. The Political Thought of Nehru/ *K.S. Bharti*
Vol. III. The Political Thought of Rabindra Nath Tagore/ *K.S. Bharti*
Vol. IV. The Political Thought of Radhakrishnan/ *K.S. Bharti*
Vol. V. The Political Thought of Vinoba/ *K.S. Bharti*
Vol. VI. The Political Thought of Aurobindo/ *K.S. Bharti*
Vol. VII. The Political Thought of Jayaprakash Narayan/ *K.S. Bharti*
Vol. VIII. The Political Thought of Vivekananda/ *K.S. Bharti*
Vol. IX. The Political Thought of Ambedkar/ *K.S. Bharti*
Vol. X. The Political Thought of M.N. Roy/ *K.S. Bharti*
Vol. XI. The Political Thought of Dadabhai Naoroji/ *Ashu Pasricha*
Vol. XII. The Political Thought of Veer Savarkar/ *Jai Narain Sharma*
Vol. XIII. The Political Thought of M.A. Jinnah/ *Jai Narain Sharma*
Vol. XIV. The Political Thought of Tej Bahadur Sapru/ *Ashu Pasricha*
Vol. XV. The Political Thought of C. Rajagopalachari/ *Ashu Pasricha*
Vol. XVI. The Political Thought of Subhas Chandra Bose/ *Ashu Pasricha*
Vol. XVII. The Political Thought of Mohammad Iqbal/ *Jai Narain Sharma*
Vol. XVIII. The Political Thought of K.B. Hedgewar/ *Jai Narain Sharma*
Vol. XIX. The Political Thought of Bhagat Singh/ *Ashu Pasricha*
Vol. XX. The Political Thought of M.S. Golwalkar/ *Jai Narain Sharma*
Vol. XXI. The Political Thought of Sir Syed Ahmed Khan/ *Jai Narain Sharma*
Vol. XXII. The Political Thought of Mahadev Govind Ranade/ *Ashu Pasricha*
Vol. XXIII. The Political Thought of Pandit Deendayal Upadhyaya/ *Jai Narain Sharma*
Vol. XXIV. The Political Thought of Lokmanya Bal Gangadhar Tilak/ *Jai Narain Sharma*
Vol. XXV. The Political Thought of Annie Besant/ *Ashu Pasricha*

Forthcoming

The Political Thought of C.R. Das/ *Ashu Pasricha*
The Political Thought of Gopal Krishna Gokhale/ *Jai Narain Sharma*
The Political Thought of Lala Lajpat Rai/ *Ashu Pasricha*
The Political Thought of Maulana Abul Kalam Azad/ *Jai Narain Sharma*
The Political Thought of Sir Pherozeshah Mehta/ *Ashu Pasricha*

CONTENTS

1

LIFE AND ACTIVITIES

Deendayal was born on September 25, 1916 in the village of Dhankia on Jaipur-Ajmer Rail line, where his maternal grandfather, Chunnilal Shukla, was working as station master. His father, Bhagwati Prasad, belonged to village Farrah (Nagla Chandrabhan) in district Mathura. He was the station master of Jalesar Road station, near Mathura. His paternal grandfather, Pandit Hariram, was a well known astrologer. When he died there was a *Hartal* in Agra and Mathura.

Bhagwati Prasad passed away when Deendayal was less than three years old. With his mother he went and stayed with his maternal grandfather. But before he was eight, he lost his mother too. Deendayal was thereafter brought up by his maternal uncle, Radha Raman Shukla, who was a railway guard on the Frontier Mail.

Deendayal was an outstanding child. He did his matric from Kalyan High School, Sikar, standing 'first class first' in the Ajmer Board examinations. He was awarded a gold medal each by the Board and the school. Two years later he stood first class first in the Intermediate examination from Birla College, Pilani. Again he got two gold medals, one from the Board and the other from the college. He did his B.A. with Mathematics from S.D. College, Kanpur in first class. Panditji joined St. John's College in Agra, to do his M.A. in Maths but left it midway and went to Allahabad where he did L.T. During all his college career he was the recipient of a monthly scholarship.

When the Rashtriya Swayamsevak Sangh came to U.P. in 1937, Deendayal was one of the first few to join it. And he stayed on to make the RSS a mighty force in that biggest State of the Union.

As soon as he had completed his studies, he decided not to take up any job. He decided, instead, to devote his life to the RSS work of national awakening and national consolidation. Beginning as a district Pracharak in Lakhimpur, U.P. in 1942, he rose within five years to be Joint Provincial Pracharak, next only to Bhaurao Deoras. He continued on this position till 1951 when his services were lent to Bharatiya Jana Sangh founded in the same year.[1]

Pandit Deendayal entered politics as the Organising Secretary of Jana Sangh in U.P. In 1968 he became president of Jana Sangh. During the 17-year period of 1951-1968, he helped Jana Sangh to stand on its own feet. He was a worker of the Rashtriya Swayamsevak Sangh from 1938 to 1951. Before joining Jana Sangh, he was the Sah-Prant Pracharak (Joint Propaganda Secretary) of RSS in UttarPradesh. His personality was shaped and his thinking was moulded by RSS. Therefore, while making a study of his political work and leadership, it will be worthwhile to understand as to how Pandit Deendayal represented the basic ideology of RSS, what were his own political perceptions as a volunteer of RSS. As the early thinking and personality of Deendayal was shaped by RSS, the texture of his leadership was different from that of others; his thinking process and political reflexes were also different from those of other political leaders.[2]

In other words, it can be said that by inducting Deendayal into the political arena, the RSS had experimented to find out as to how the leadership and personality of a person, shaped in RSS mould, would develop in the world outside the RSS, and what new dimensions would it acquire. For this reason, Deendayal entered politics as seeker after truth and a creative thinker and not as a seeker after power. His goal and his role were well defined.[3]

Panditji knew that a party does not become strong only by its thoughts, development, expression and propaganda. He intended that each worker must be properly moulded, that there must be a team of such workers on every level and that through the efforts of such teams must be done contacting,,awakening, education of the masses as also their organisation and movement. Through all this he hoped, on the one hand, to spread the party roots deep and wide, and on the other hand, to develop the party branches to spread and also to reach higher and higher towards the goal. Propaganda is important; but more important is education and what is still more important for the workers is to give them good *Sanskaras* (Sanskara is inculcating good qualities and principles). Shri Aurobindo says, "Inspiration is real work. Let a truly inspiring word be uttered and it will breathe life into dry bones. Let the inspiring life be lived and it will produce workers by thousands."[4]

In order to impart proper *sanskaras* to workers, the best means is the pure life of the leader and his constant, informal .and family like relationship with the workers. For this are necessary leader's contact with each worker, free discussions in small groups, and study camps. And in addition are necessary large propaganda in newspapers, the use of periodicals run by the friends and of the party's propaganda literature for the education of workers. The knowledge of each worker's mind, his motivation, and mutual personal relationships of workers; from this the ability to take correct decision in assigning work to each one; knowledge of each worker's circumstances and difficulties and the ability and promptness in guiding him and assessing him ; in case of the workers of inner-core the confidence, arising out of actual behaviour of the leader, that justice will be done to everyone on the basis of assessment of his work, his idealism, his qualities and abilities, and not on the basis of leader's personal likes and dislikes; inculcating in the workers' minds life-values conducive to the goal and the attitude of mind which considers things not from a personal but organisational point of view; elastic discipline which properly balances individual initiative and organisational restrictions; absence of insistence on personal conveniences as also absence of any compromise on principles—the inculcation of these two; the willingness of the workers to work for a very long time with courage and without hope of any quick success because they have been told that their task is in a way, lunacy, like falling in love with the stars; the credibility about the party, not arising from mere talking but born out of the actual behaviour of the leader as seen through the workers' contact with him; the party members themselves; the first circle of party sympathisers; the circle of people formed from among these sympathisers and constituting the zone of benevolent neutrality, these last four forming the infrastructure of the party; all these have to be attended to.

Panditji used to say that without this infrastructure, any attempt at trying to strengthen a party by mere high propaganda and image-building is just day-dreaming. When infrastructure is ready, high propaganda may be necessary depending on circumstances. But such propaganda cannot be done without this infrastructure. Even if men and money are available, they can't be properly utilised without this infrastructure. It was in this scientific way that Deendayal laid the foundation of the party. He was also a skilled organiser; but his eminence as a great thinker paled him as a great organiser. One can say that his capacity to think did injustice to his capacity as an organiser.

An important part in the process of organisation, is the creation of a cooperative team of workers at every level. All the members of this team are co-travellers on the path to the goal; all are fired by the same ideal. They love and confide in each other as they tread a common path to a common ideal. Such a cooperative team has been significantly termed 'Master-mind Group' by Napoleon Hill. The real strength of the organisation lies in the numerical growth of this group as also in each individual's growing faith in the ideal, and qualitative improvement of personal virtues. Panditji, was ever desirous that such a group should be formed at each level and that it should ever grow, both numerically and qualitatively.[5]

Rather than using gatherings, sessions or public functions, he used opportunities of informal individual discussions with each worker at Seminars for moulding the workers. Maharashtra workers remember the 10-day all-India study camp which began on 27th June 1959.[6] Earlier from 8th August to 18th August 1957, there was held an eleven day all-Bharat study camp at Vilaspur in Chhattisgarh.[7] In all these camps, special stress was laid on the moulding of workers. The various meetings also stressed this aspect. The fruits of all this had begun to show in Panditji's life-time. At all levels such teams of workers had started forming and the numerical strength was increasing and quality was improving.

Panditji was a strong protagonist of democracy. But his brand of democracy was not of the Western model. He was for democracy consistent with Bharatiya tradition. Though Bharat is the largest democracy, he was sorry that it is not the best. For successful democracy people must be educated. The effectiveness of party organisation and people's movement will ultimately depend on the level of people's education. People's education is not mere propaganda; the core of party-propaganda is the praise of the party, and the denunciation of other parties. But he did not think that democracy can succeed thereby. Along the education of the workers, he thought it necessary to educate the masses. He felt anxious about the future of democracy because the number of parties and leaders who think in this constructive way is ever diminishing. It was a speciality of Panditji that he could adjust his talk to the level of the listeners. As an example, consider what he said, while talking about 'what *is Sanskriti'* to an uneducated audience. He said, "It is natural to yawn—this is *Prakriti* (nature). Purposely making queer faces to yawn and making large sound while yawning is *Vikriti* (perversion), but yawning without making sound or making faces and holding a kerchief before the mouth *is Sanskriti* (culture):"[8] He could thus express even a difficult subject in simple words. He was a great mass-educator.

For three decades he was touring. Most of his time he spent in vehicles—from bullock cart and passenger train to fast aeroplanes.

If he were accompanied by an Image-Builder, the latter would have provided impressive figures in the American style: how many lakhs of miles he travelled, how many crores of people were contacted directly and indirectly, how many days would be necessary to run the tapes of all he talked etc. A lot of such data is published in America by companies which take contracts of propaganda at the time of Presidential election. Fortunately, Panditji did not have such an Image-Builder. The original Image itself being bright, no such Image-Builder was necessary. 'A naturally beautiful thing does not have to be beautified' or 'Anything beautifies the naturally beautiful'. Also artificial image-building would not suit his temperament.

Of what Panditji may have said in this long continuous touring, is at least a hundredth part available now? There are so many *bouddhiks* (lectures) in RSS, so many public lectures, so many meetings, so many personal talks besides personal confidential talks with many! If all this were available, it would have been a vast store-house from which to draw for the new generation and for new workers. However, efforts of researchers should be directed towards collecting as much material as possible, which will benefit the nation.

Panditji was self-effacing; he belonged to the tradition of those who would say, 'After my death not even a small monument should be erected in my memory.'[9] There are so many *Rishis* who are the authors of Vedic Sooktas and Upanishads. We only know their names; but in the cases of how many of them do we know about their lives ? It is impossible to expect a man of his stature to write his memoirs like Lloyd George or Churchill, or write his partial autobiography like Pandit Nehru or Mussolini or Hitler. Also he is imbued with the *samskara* of RSS.

He was so simple in his habits that his banyans (undergarment) would be in shreds before he agreed to replace them. He did not boast about *swadeshi* but he never bought *videshi*.

Dr. Mookerji was so impressed with Deendayal's organising ability after the Kanpur session that he said, 'if only he had two Deendayals he could transform the political face of India'.[10] Though he rose to be a great leader, Deendayal was a believer and follower of simple living; he even washed his clothes with his own hands.

Unfortunately Dr. Mookerji died soon, and the responsibility of transforming the political face of India fell on Deendayal himself. He achieved this quietly with a distinction that startled the country. This was evident by the results of 1967 elections. He described it as the Second Revolution—the first one being the Independence of India. Jana Sangh emerged a Number Two Party in the country. It was clear that its emergence as the First Party was a matter of only a few years.

As editor of *Panchajanya* (Weekly) and *Swadesh* (daily) in Lucknow, he not only edited the papers, he would compose the matter, tend the machine and even act as binder and despatcher, whenever necessary! On one occasion, in the late forties, he wrote *Chandragupta Maurya*—a novelette about that hero—in Hindi—at one stretch of 16 hours.[11] Later he wrote a biography of

Shankaracharya, also in Hindi.[12] Later still he translated RSS founder Dr. Hedgewar's definitive biography from Marathi into Hindi.

Though very ordinary in appearance, he was extraordinary in everything else—in the sweep of his ideas, in the utter sincerity of his words, in the tireless persistence of his work and in the sheer purity of his life.

Deendayal who became the General Secretary of the Jana Sangh soon after its inception continued till a few months before he died. Presidents came and went but the General Secretary remained. He built up the party-worker by worker, state by state. As Atal Behari Vajpayee put it, he was not an M.P. himself, but he had made all the persons of Jana Sangh M.Ps. And yet nobody ever heard him speak of himself or his efforts. The word 'I' seemed to be taboo with him. As Yagyadutt put it, his life was a sacred *triveni* in which *tamas* was as non-existent as Saraswati at the *Sangam,* while *rajas* and *satva* were deep and wide as Yumuna and Ganga.[13]

In 1963, Panditji was invited to visit the U.S.A. But the thoughtless Reserve Bank would not issue him 'P' form! It was at Nehruji's personal intervention that he got the form. He took this opportunity to visit U.K., West Germany and East Africa also. He made a great impression on the Indian communities in London, Nairobi and elsewhere.

Panditji's principal subject in college had been Mathematics. And his first love had been Sanskrit. But as soon as he entered public life he realised the importance of Economics. He thoroughly studied the subject till he had understood it better than any economic theoretician. He read the various plans with more attention than perhaps any other politician or economist. His most original contribution to Indian economic thought was *Integral Humanism*: the relating of the four *purusharthas—dharma, artha, kama, moksha*—to the socio-economic problems of today.

Only a few weeks before he was done to death on February 11,1968, in circumstances still shrouded in mystery, Deendayal presided over the historic Calicut session of the Jana Sangh. Commenting on the great session, the *Mathrubhoomi*—the biggest paper of India—wrote that for three days it looked as if the Ganga had changed its course and began to flow through Kerala.[14] Jana

Sangh had arrived in the South with a big bang. It was in this great hour that he was murdered—like Swami Dayanand Saraswati, Swami Shraddhanand and Mahatma Gandhi before him.

REFERENCES

1. Upadhyaya, Deendayal, *Political Diary* (New Delhi: Suruchi Prakashan), 1992, p. 7.
2. Kelkar, B.K., *Pandit Deendayal Upadhyaya, Ideology and Perception*, Part III, *Political Thought* (New Delhi: Suruchi Prakashan), 1991, p. 10.
3. *Ibid.*
4. Thengadi, D.B., *Pandit Deendayal Upadhyaya, Ideology and Perception*, Part I, *An Inquest* (New Delhi: Suruchi Prakashan), 1991, pp. 27-28.
5. *Ibid.*
6. Resolutions passed at Bharatiya Pratinidhi Sabha Session and the Working Committee, 1960.
7. *Ibid.*
8. Thengadi, D.B., *Pandit Deendayal Upadhyaya, Ideology and Perception*, Part I, *An Inquest, op. cit. p. 30.*
9. Upadhyaya, *Deendayal, Political Diary, op. cit.*
10. *Ibid.*, p. 8.
11. Upadhyaya, Deendayal, *Samrat Chandragupta* (New Delhi: Suruchi Prakashan), 1968.
12. Upadhyaya, Deendayal, *Jagat Guru Shankrachariya* (New Delhi: Suruchi Prakashan), 1968.
13. Upadhyaya, Deendayal, *Political Diary, op. cit.*, p. 9.
14. *Ibid.*

2

IDEOLOGY AND PERCEPTION

Deendayal was assigned the work of assisting Dr. Mookherji by M.S. Golwalkar because he knew that Deendayal possessed all the qualities of a good organiser, viz. high intellect, capability, sweetness of speech, organising capacity, mental and emotional balance. Golwalkar had watched the development of Deendayal as a volunteer. His qualities as a thinker were described by him after his demise thus: "One notable quality of Deendayal was that while expounding a subject in speech or writing, he always kept close to the main ideal. He never gave up this habit. It was not in his nature to look at a question merely in the context of immediate problems. I knew him as a person who went to the root of every matter. While speaking on or writing about a matter of immediate importance, he never lost sight of the enduring truth."[1]

It was a leader of such mental capability and discipline who was needed, a leader who could provide a new philosophy to the country, keeping in view the problems facing it. Not only this, he was a person who was totally devoid of egotism and who had wholly merged his identity with the society. For him, politics was a new field of national service. He was a living symbol of the ideal conceived by Samartha Ramdas in *Dasbodh*:

> "Discard all pleasures. Cath this opportunity.
> Secure your kingdom. That is your duty."[2]

Deendayal built up Jana Sangh in a manner and provided it with a national outlook so as to enable it to come to power in the future. He became the theorist of Jana Sangh; his character and organisational ability were ideals for the Party.

Theoretical Base

Jana Sangh was formulating its ideology in a three-fold manner : (1) thinking about the decisions taken by the Congress Party; (2) providing Bharatiya outlook for the basic concepts adopted by independent Bharat; and (3) providing a new ideology to the country.

The Congress government had taken three important decisions: The first was to follow the policy of neutrality by not joining any power bloc or military alliance. The second related to adopting planned economy, and the third to adopting mixed economy. Jana Sangh presented (formulated) its own views on these matters and put them before the government and the people in the form of resolutions from time to time.

All these formulations originated from Deendayal in all respects, he was the Guru of Jana Sangh. The idea of 'Integral Humanism', as conceived by Deendayal, was formally adopted by Jana Sangh at its Vijayawada Conference held in 1965. Jana Sangh's policy in regard to language, culture, Bharat-Pak relations, formation of coalition governments, elections, economic matters, Five Year Plans and decentralisation etc. were formulated by Deendayal. In his introduction to the booklet containing a collection of resolutions passed by Jana Sangh on economic matters, Atal Behari Vajpayee had described Deendayal as being the architect of the economic policies of Jana Sangh.[3]

In view of the above, it would be useful to investigate as to what was the basis of the policies adopted by Bhartiya Jana Sangh on various matters. Such an investigation would not only be inspiring but provide guideline in view of the fact that all those problems are not only unresolved, they have become even more complex. There is an all round confusion because of the prevailing ad hocism. A politician's thinking is limited to matters of immediate interest. No one has the courage to speak the bitter truth in a democracy with the result that politicians mostly adopt a populist approach. Such politics was foreign to the nature of Deendayal. The guiding principles of his thinking were the good of the people and the nation, and the cultural values. Formulating the policies of a party on the basis of such guiding principles is not always beneficial with the result that mostly policies are generally based on populist slogans. Such policies do not look to the future and do not take into account the reality. Deendayal's style of thinking was to go to the root of a matter; his thinking was based on practical experience. As he was entrusted with the responsibility of drafting the economic resolutions of Bhartiya Jana Sangh, he always tried to understand the sufferings and problems of the common man through direct contact with such people. It would be interesting to recall an incident in this context, which throws light on his style of functioning in this regard.

The incident relates to Lucknow where he had gone in connection with the movement against cow-slaughter. One day, he wanted to have his hair cut. He had set apart one hour for this purpose. It was 7 A.M. but the barber had not turned up. He went to one or two hair cutting saloons but they were over-crowded. Then he saw a barber sitting idle on the foot path with no customer. He sat down before him and got his hair cut. On return, his workers asked him, "Where did you get this hair cut?" He laughed and replied, "In a mobile saloon; the barber was in need of a client and I was in need of a barber." While he was getting his hair cut, he had been enquiring from the barber all about his financial condition. It was in this way that he used to make himself acquainted with the condition of rickshaw pullers, push cartmen and slum dwellers, etc. He always tried to gain first hand knowledge about the sufferings and difficulties of the common man by making direct contact with him. To understand the country's economic problems, he read books, but studied Bharatiya life at first hand.[4]

Study of Established Ideologies

The chief aim of economic development is the happiness of the common man. As such, Deendayal undertook a comparative study of the various economic theories and their practical application in India and other countries. Nanaji Deshmukh, who was a close colleague of Deendayal, has written in this context, "Nationalism, democracy, socialism, communism are theories based on equality. But none of these theories is perfect. In practice, they are contradictory to one another. Nationalism can pose danger to world peace; democracy is eroded by capitalism leading to exploitation; socialism, while it destroys capitalism, also destroys democracy in the process and puts individual freedom in danger. So, today, the western countries are vexed with the problem of bringing about harmony among these ideologies so as to make them complementary to one another. Deendayal was keenly aware of the need of having a practicable and over-all philosophy of life which should be relevant to the time we live in. His thoughts and studies were directed towards evolving such a philosophy. The result of these labours was the birth of the concept of 'Integral Humanism'. Jana Sangh adopted it as an ideology. Deendayal thought about theories and men without prejudices. He tried to investigate the real worth of every doctrine; this was his speciality."[5]

In this manner, Deendayal commenced his ideological research. Apart from being influenced by thinkers like Swami Dayanand, Lokmanya Tilak, Dr. Hedgewar, he also had the benefit of Golwalkar's guidance. Golwalkar and Deendayal, both used to consult each other and often held ideological discussions. Golwalkar had once given him a book entitled '*Daishik Shastra*'. It was a book written at the time when Lokmanya Tilak was alive. Tilak had, in fact, written to its author Badrishah Thuldharia and praised the book. Deendayal used this as a reference book while propounding the concept of 'Integral Humanism'. The book had been originally written in Hindi. After going through its manuscript, Tilak had written to the author, "I have been happy to go through your 'Daishik Shastra'. You and I have exactly common views." The subject matter of this book is a treatise on patriotism. The concepts of Chiti (consciousness) and '*Virat*' (as big as Cosmos), were explained by Thuldharia in this book. Deendayal once again gave currency to these two terms. The theory that the identity of Bharat as a nation is known from time immemorial, that its national unity lies in its cultural unity, and that the consciousness of this unity should be made to live again in the Bharatiya people, was adopted by Deendayal as the central idea of his concept.[6] In the first issue of

'Rashtra Dharma' published in July-August 1947, he had written an article about Bharatiya Culture which was entitled *'Bharatiya Rashtra-dhara ka Punya-Pravah.'* The main contention of this article was that Indian Nationalism is founded on culture. We should once again invoke this integrated culture.[7] Similarly, in a review of the book entitled *'Daishik Shastra'*, which was published in *Panchajanya*, dated 24th August 1968, under the caption 'Bharat of Lokmanya's dreams', he had broached the idea of Integral Humanism. He had written, "Those who are for nationalism, harmony and perfection believe that there should be harmony between Western materialism and the spiritualism of Bharat. Life cannot be divided into two separate parts—materialism and spiritualism. The values which inspire man to improve society through his conduct emanate from a motive force which is spiritual. A harmonious social life leads to the inculcation of such values. A Society is not like a machine and cannot be built merely by assembling various components. If we are not to adopt the material path of the West, then what is our own path ? We do not know our own path nor do we have the confidence to find it. Hence, we fall a prey to the Western publicity and start copying the West. In writing *'Daishik Shastra'*, Badrishah Thuldharia was inspired by *'Karmarga Shastra'* written by Lokmanya Tilak. By advocating Karma-Yoga on the basis of Gita, Lokmanya Tilak had diverted the spiritualism of Bharat from *Nivritti* (inaction) towards *Pravritti* (action). He had pulled out the eternal values of Bharatiya culture from the caves of the Himalayas and brought them to the open planes of Bharat and provided a new source of energy to the national movement. *'Daishik Shastra'* and *'Karmayoga Shastra'* are the two books which are supplementary to each other. A person dedicated to the work of nation-building must go through both these books. The two books will provide us solutions to all our problems."[8]

Deendayal was convinced that these two books contained the basic ideas of a national philosophy of life for Bharat.

Adya-Shankaracharya—His Dharma Renaissance

While exploring the mental and ideological background of Deendayal, we shall have to go far back in time. In a character sketch of Adya-Shankaracharya written by him, Deendayal has analysed as to how Adya-Shankaracharya met the challenge of Buddhism, how he re-established Vedic Dharma all over Bharat and how he was able to bring about a change in keeping with the time without sacrificing the traditions. He had expressed his views on this subject in an article in the first issue (July-August 1947) of the monthly '*Rashtra Dharma*'. From this essay we can guess his own line of thinking, for, although he was deeply rooted in tradition, he also had a great craving for change. Consequently, he was always exploring as to how changes had been brought about in the Hindus in the past and who were instrumental in bringing about these changes. In his article on *Adya-Shankaracharya and Gautam Buddha*, Deendayal has said, "Shankaracharya is a shining example of the existence of harmonious tendency in Hindu Dharma. He understood the revolt of Buddha. He had properly understood the changed times. Buddha's revolt had, no doubt, harmed the country. In those days, thinkers about Dharma were mainly faced with the question, how to make Vedic Dharma strong in all respects and how to change it to suit the times. In so far as the eternal values of life are concerned, it was accepted and insisted upon in Hindu Dharma that in order to bring about fullness in our lives we should not hesitate to change with times the means to the attainment of such fullness. Shankaracharya brought new changes while protecting the ancient values. In so doing, he did not harm the soul of the Nation. The external form of Hindu Dharma underwent a change but its inner form remained unchanged. In his period there was a strong tendency to bring about harmony between those sects and religious beliefs which gave strength to national feeling. Most of the credit for bringing about such a harmony must go to Shankaracharya. Shankaracharya, must also be given credit for the confluence of *Karma, Bhakti* and *Jynana* (action, devotion and knowledge) which was brought about in his time."[9]

The Indian Terminology

While Deendayal was engaged in his enquiries about conceptions relating to democracy, socialism etc. and their implications, the touch stone by which he judged the merits of these conceptions was the Bharatiya values of life. The central idea of his thinking was that the ancient values have to be recalled and redefined again and again in changed situation. As such, he always kept in his mind the ideological conceptions of great men like Shankaracharya, Lokmanya Tilak and Swami Dayanand. A change is moulded by changed circumstances as also, to a great extent, by the *sanskaras* on mind and intellect. Therefore, while studying the thoughts of Deendayal, it is necessary to analyse his thinking process. Reference to the foregoing has been made only from this point of view. In his book '*Daishik Shastra*', Thuldharia has considered the questions relating to patriotism, nationalism, freedom and Bharat only in the context of ancient thinking. For example, in the first chapter of the book entitled 'Patriotism', while presenting important points for consideration, reference has been made to the situation prevailing in India. Reference has also been made to the tendency, prevailing in Britain, of subserving the interest of the country in disregard of the personal interests. Words like *'Chiti'* and *'Virat'* have also been made use of in this context. All this has been done to define the contemporary questions in Bharatiya terms in the context of ancient thoughts. Words acquire currency when they are used to express a particular concept. In such concepts, individual and social principles are inherent. It was because of this that Deendayal once again gave currency to the words, '*Chiti*' and *'Virat'*. Not only this, while accepting the ancient conceptions of reality, he gave new definitions to those old formulations. This was Deendayal's ideological achievement. It is because of this that in his expositions we again and again come across ancient terms and contexts. Each time when Deendayal discussed the Indian situation or the new Western experiments or formulations, he gave evidence of this awareness.

In the light of '*Chiti*', for example, in the November-December 1950 issue of *Rashtra Dharma* he wrote an article entitled *Chiti*. In this article Deendayal had explained in detail the idea of nation's soul and its importance in national reconstruction. This article was written after India became free. It gives an indication of the direction in which his mind was moving. Independence of India was an incident which ushered a new age. But till the attainment of freedom, a simple equation had become prevalent that patriotism only meant opposition of the British. We proceeded on the presumption that the basic cause of all our economic and other ills was British rule. But nobody thought of giving a constructive and emotional shape to patriotism. But Deendayal said, "Patriotism is implied in the concept of nation. Why do all of us think about the nation ? It is because we have the feeling that the glory of the nation includes our own glory. But are we inspired, in our patriotism, only by such a selfish consideration ? Had this been so, there would have been no difference between the unity of dacoits and our unity based on selfish interests. Patriotism means getting submerged in the national social entity. Feeling of affinity for such a national social entity is patriotism. Such an affinity is born from the feeling that the individual and the society have a common soul. Like an individual, nation also has a soul. The existence of such a soul makes our nation one. This soul of the nation has been termed 'Chiti' by our thinkers. Every nation has its own *Chiti;* it is this *Chiti* which is the symbol of nationalism and gives a different identity to the culture of every nation. Literature, art, religion, language are all manifestations of this *chiti.* Just as all parts of the body remain joined together because of the existence of *Atma* (soul), in the same way culture, religion, language etc. are related to this national soul. All draw sustenance from this soul. The social unity formed in a particular society and the collective entity of the society owe their existence to this *'Chiti'*. Destruction of *Chiti* results in the fall of the nation. If we want Bharat to rise, we shall have to reveal to its people the *Chiti* or the true soul of Bharat. We shall not be able to restore the glory of our nation merely by taking recourse to its physical adornment. The objective of constructive patriotism, relevant to the present times, shall have to be pursued by us."[10]

Virat—the National Active Force

Chiti, the national soul, creates life's active force in a nation. This national active force has been called *Virat* by Panditji. It pulsates in the entire nation and success of democracy depends on it.

Nature, Dharma and Culture

The ideology of Deendayal is based not only on the idea *of 'Chiti'* and *'Virat'* but also on his postulates relating to Dharma, Nature, culture and concepts of 'I' and 'we'. The basic ideology of Deendayal may be called sociological. However, it is not an ideology akin to the Western sociological ideologies. But the questions he has discussed are social. Nationalism has also been considered by him in the context of culture and Dharma. By way of our illustration, one may quote the article written by him under the caption 'Nature, Dharma and Culture' in *Panchajanya* (13th July 1959). In this article, 'culture' has been analysed in the following words :

"The individual and the universal, both are related to culture. Culture is basically social in character. It is through culture that the soul of a society manifests itself. Although society is like the all pervading Brahma, it has, in every place, an individuality of its own which is manifested through the individual. In the same way, culture is a social quality, manifested in each individual, comprising a society. According to the Hindu thought, individual and society are inseparable entities. According to the Bharatiya way of thinking, the existence of individual apart from the society is not conceivable.

"It is the job of culture to bring about harmony between the interests of the society and the individual and to ensure that there is no confrontation between the two. The body, mind and senses of man function according to his nature and follow some rules, called *Dharma.* When there is violation of these rules or when the individual commits some excess, we call it perversion. It is necessary to avoid such an excess or perversion. This function is performed by *Dharma.* Therefore, it is through *Dharma* that culture functions. *Dharma* holds the society together, rather, the existence of a regulated society is possible only because of *Dharma.* Just as the body of man remains free of disease so long as he follows certain rules of eating and physical exercise etc., in the same way the society functions in an orderly manner through the observance of *Dharma;* the behaviours of individuals with one another become smooth by Dharma.

"Thus, *Dharma* has a social content. No individual can create everything that he needs, on his own. For this he needs the help of others; there has to be a give and take; avoidance of confrontation in mutual behaviour has also to be ensured. It is for this reason that the individual and social behaviour have to be regulated by *Dharma*. This is called sustenance of society.

"Culture performs the function of creating an atmosphere in which the individual is not selfish and behaves in a manner which is not anti-social. This is the second stage of *Dharma*. All human behaviour is not based on self-interest. One has to take into account the interest of others as well. The inspiration to adopt such a behaviour comes to the individual from culture."[11]

In substance, Deendayal considered culture to be a code of individual and social behaviour. Hence, it was in this wider and deeper context that Deendayal talked of the establishment of *Dharma-rajya* in Bharat. It is clear from this that the thinking of Deendayal was basic in approach. He looked at socialism, democracy, humanism etc. from this basic point of view. Hence his analysis of every concept was purely Bharatiya in nature. He never accepted a concept only because it was novel nor rejected it because it was foreign. He used to analyse any new idea in his own critical way before drawing conclusions. In this way, Deendayal was a constructive critic and a creative thinker.

Socialism, Democracy and Humanism

Deendayal made a critical study of contemporary ideologies from the Bharatiya point of view, drew his own conclusions therefrom and presented them to the people. He was in search of a total philosophy of life, which he later presented in the form of Integral Humanism. Even before this, however, he had discussed this ideology in the context of socialism, democracy and humanism in *Panchajanya*. Apart from presenting his views on this subject from time to time in the study camps of RSS, he had also invited Dr. Ram Manohar Lohia to speak on socialism. Dr. Lohia accepted the invitation and spoke on the subject.

Deendayal used to say, "It has become a fashion with people these days to style themselves as socialists and the political parties vie with one another in adopting the ideology of socialism." Referring to this tendency, Deendayal had said, "In Europe socialism is prevalent in various forms. Hitler, Mussolini, Stalin, all used to call themselves socialists. In India also, we have all varieties of socialists. Some leaders talk of giving a Bharatiya form to European socialism. In his last days, M.N. Roy gave up socialism and tried to propagate Radical Humanism."[12]

In a different context Swami Vivekananda had also said, "I am a socialist."[13] What inspires every socialist is the sympathy for starving human beings and the desire to give them equal status and dignity. This desire, no doubt, is commendable. It is natural for any body within a human heart to develop socialistic feelings on seeing pain, suffering, torture, exploitation, hunger, slavery and poverty all round. But socialism does not stop there. It also wants to do away with these miseries, it has analysed poverty and diagnosed the ills. For this, a socialist has to borrow from Marxism. Even those who are opposed to Marxism cannot but accept the Marxist analysis. However, the history of the period following the Bolshevik revolution till today has demonstrated that Marxist ideology is not perfect.

Democracy is the first casualty in socialism. Marx has envisaged a classless society. He had also visualised the establishment of the 'dictatorship of the proletariat' in the transition period. However, in practice, the developments took a different turn. The political freedom achieved by man again slipped out of his hands. Prince Kropotkin had clearly admitted in his letter of 28th April 1919, addressed to workers of Europe, that the communist concept of developing a people's State from out of party dictatorship or iron rule would ultimately remain unrealised.[14]

This failure of Marxist pattern has brought into focus the concept of democratic socialism. But even in a socialist system, the means of production are owned by the State. The State, however, does not want to limit its supremacy to the economic field but tries to attack political rights as well. Thus the guns of socialism are turned towards democracy. Socialism and democracy cannot co-exist, just as a lion and a goat cannot live together. The whole thing becomes even more complicated if an attempt is made to take into consideration the cultural and social set up of a society while bringing about economic development. It seems impossible to resolve this complication. This socialist dilemma has also affected capitalism where, in place of socialism, the idea of welfare State has emerged.

The mental capacity to remedy the errors is inherent in a democratic set-up, but the socialist system does not possess such flexibility. The die-hard socialist wants to keep himself away from independent thinking just as the followers of a religion based on blind faith do. The communist dictionary contains a number of abusive epithets for independent thinkers. However, a thinking individual cannot exist in a state of thoughtlessness.

Today, Bharatiya socialism gives stress on nationalisation. It is, no doubt, true that in an undeveloped economy government has to keep certain industries under its control; the individual capitalists cannot be given a free hand. Competition has to be put under check. But it is necessary to have a proper balance between the two sectors. Democracy and socialism are two different systems. They are not compatible with each other. According to us, these two concepts are not mutually alternative. Both of these systems are only means and not an end in themselves. It is, therefore, necessary that we first identify our goal and then choose the approach to achieve it.

Slavery to Machines

If we want to protect humanity, we shall have first to liberate it from the slavery of machines. Today, it is not man who controls the machine; rather, it is the machine which controls man. At the back of this love for machine is man's lust for increasing his needs and satisfying them. Hence, while thinking of human life in its totality, we shall have to take into consideration production, distribution and consumption together. We shall have to develop an economic order (system) wherein production and consumption are both achieved in the context of a meaningful life.

Hinduism is Essential

"Only the Hindu philosophy, based on the four-fold objective, comprising *Dharma,* wealth, gratification of senses and liberation, can save us from the present crisis. The solution of world's problems lies in Hinduism and not in socialism. Hinduism is a philosophy which does not tie man down to a single rigid frame. We should not confuse this philosophy of Hinduism with the decadent ritualism. It is also wrong to think that Hinduism is opposed to scientific progress. Science and technology should be used in conformity with our social and cultural life. We shall have to have technology to suit our political, economic, social and ideological needs. Hence, our objectives should be, rule based on Dharma, democracy, social equality and economic decentralisation. We need an 'ism' which includes these elements. You may call it by any name, Hinduism or humanism."[15]

This analysis by Deendayal is not negative; it is a concept which can guide us on the right path. Deendayal judged the economic, social and political events in the light of this principle. Economic planning as also economic thoughts and economic objectives are also included therein. His economic thinking also is concerned about the protection and conservation of human and cultural values. He did not confine himself to economic analysis.

Deendayal planned to reach beyond communism but by democratic path and without giving up eternal values in life. In his time, the ideological challenge from communism was strong. It was, therefore, necessary for him to lay emphasis on economic policies. Deendayal's economic thoughts can be found in his treatise entitled '*Economic Policy of Bharat : New Direction of Development*'. The ideas contained therein are briefly stated below :

In India, Dharma regulates life. However, this Dharma is not only spiritual in character. Chanakya has said, 'The basis of happiness is Dharma. The basis of Dharma is *Artha*.' In other words, happiness should be based on Dharma. But Dharma cannot survive without wealth. Here Dharma signifies the system which holds the society together. Wealth should not influence life in a manner that it becomes the end rather than the means of our life. If this happens, man becomes a slave of sense-pleasures and loses his abilities and ideals in life. In such a situation, the values of conduct also undergo a change and there is no longer any insistence on purity of means; conduct is no longer based on Dharma, and greed for wealth becomes supreme.

While wealth should not hold its sway on our life, at the same time, there should be no shortage of it. The social status of the man, comfortable maintenance, his political importance and social behaviour are all dependent on wealth. Poverty leads to moral degradation of man. The object of desire of a poor man is only wealth with the result that he loses his balance in life.

It is for this reason that the concept of a balanced economy for Bharat has been supported, which would seek to eradicate the dominance of wealth and also the lack or shortage of it. It has been called *'Arthayam'*. In order to evolve such an economic system, it would be necessary to change social standards. A social system based on the concept of wealth alone would be undesirable. An economic being will only build a society based on the concept of wealth. Therefore, in principle, the concept of man as an economic being is wrong. A soldier exists only for valour and a seeker of knowledge considers knowledge much above wealth. Valour and knowledge cannot be valued in terms of money or labour. The dignity of labour does not depend on the amount of wealth earned by it; rather it depends on the conformity of labour with Dharma and the objective of labour. The values in Western and Bharatiya philosophy differ from each other in this respect, As such, the Western economic system is not useful for Bharat, as the values in the two systems are different and even contradictory to each other. Bharatiya values are related to Dharma, whereas the Western values are related to economics.

The Influence of Western Economics

It follows, therefore, that Bharat should follow a wholly different path for its development. We have been so much influenced by the concepts of Western economists—Marx and Marshall—that we cannot come out of their influence ! Our economists only follow the Western economic theories. They do not put forward Bharatiya economic theory. The idea of Gandhian economy has come before us only in the shape of a movement. The Gandhian thinkers did point out the evils of the Western economic system but they failed to spell out a new Bharatiya economic system. Similarly, there is a large number of economists here who are protagonists of Western economics and have vested interest in Western industrial system The two are complementary to each other. The planning system adopted by the government is also not Bharatiya, with the result that Bharat has all along been exploited even after independence. Our industrialists and entrepreneurs are only acting as agents of the Western exploitative system. Our Swadeshi movement has only been confined to Khadi cap, whereas everything else is foreign.

Criticism of Planning

Deendayal's criticism of Bharatiya planning system was always important. Criticising the Second Five Year Plan he had said, "The Second Plan is basically non-Bharatiya. It has not taken into consideration the special features of Bharatiya social system. Economic reconstruction is not a castle to be built in the air. Self-reliance should be the basic concept of our planning. The industrial development of one part of the world cannot be imposed on some other part. We should, have our own concept about agriculture and industry. Instead of importing technology, we should invent a new technology which suits our situation. We need a technology which would provide for total employment and would remove the disparity in incomes. By so doing, we shall be able to raise the standard of living of the people. Modern technology, in the West is also being developed along these lines. But the Second Five Year Plan here is based on pre-recession technology and economic concepts."[16]

In this article, Deendayal has also suggested changes in the procedure and the structure of Planning Commission and the National Development Council. It was his view that "the period of the Plan should be increased. The stages of development in the Second Plan should be changed. The Plan consists of many development projects which are indivisible. Any reduction in such projects is not only harmful but also difficult. Many a time, there is a shortage of funds which necessitates change in priorities of development. It is, therefore, not possible to confine a plan to a five year period. Economic development is a continuous process and, therefore, plans for economic development cannot be confined to the fixed limits of time. Fixation of goals leads to higher plan expenditure. Non-achievement of goals leads to disappointment. Moreover, the Five Year Plans in India are linked with elections which are held after every five years. If the period of the plans is changed, then it would be possible to get the cooperation and participation of the people. The government should not make it a question of prestige and should accept this change. The discussions held in the National Development Council in May last were devoid of realism and a sense of responsibility. In Bharat, planning is not based on commitment and a sense of responsibility; it has become a political tool. Hence, first of all, it is necessary to reorganise the Planning Commission. The composition of the National Development Council should also be changed. Planning should reach the village level. There must be all-party advisory councils. The plan should be directly based on actual economic condition and not on a particular ideology".[17] In this article, Deendayal also mentioned the fact that in the guiding principles of the. plan for economic development prepared by the British in 1948, the factual political as well as economic situation were both taken into consideration.

National Objectives of Bharatiya Economic System

What should be the objectives of the Bharatiya economic system? Discussing this question Deendayal had stated, "Our country has achieved independence after a long effort. Therefore, we should provide for a system which would protect this freedom. This should be our first goal. Secondly, we should not adopt economic planning which would endanger or obstruct our democratic system. Our third goal is with reference to our cultural values which are not only very useful for our own national life but also useful for the entire world. As such, these values have to be protected. If we achieve economic affluence after losing our cultural values then such an affluence would prove useless. Our fourth goal should be to acquire the military capability for self-defence. The fifth goal should be economic self-reliance. A nation which is economically dependent on another nation, loses its self-respect. A nation without self-respect can never protect its freedom. For protecting political freedom, it is necessary to have economic freedom. For economic freedom, economic self-reliance is a prerequisite. The sixth goal is an economic order wherein a job is ensured to everyone in the same way as the right to vote is ensured to every adult. Minimum wages suitable for the job, fair earning and their fair distribution is also necessary in the interest of society. For this, it is necessary to provide a ceiling on incomes. Freedom of consumption cannot be allowed to remain unlimited. The industrialists interpret individual freedom or individual enterprise to mean their own freedom. We do not want the freedom of a few Tatas and Birlas; we want freedom for the millions of human beings. Therefore, we are opposed to centralisation. In the capitalist system real individual freedom gradually disappears and economic power gets concentrated in the hands of a handful of persons. In the socialist system this power becomes a part of the State power and is ultimately weilded by the bureaucracy, with the result that human life is reduced to being a machine. In both the systems man is considered only to be a means and not a human being. Therefore, we shall have to free ourselves from the hold of both, socialism and capitalism, and adopt humanism. Technology should also be utilised for the benefit of man. For this, it is necessary to have a decentralised economic system. Man can be developed only when he is provided with suitable work after duly taking into consideration his needs and his qualities. This is possible only in a decentralised economic system. Once a big industrial unit is set up, it cannot be closed down without giving due thought to many considerations. Hence, it is necessary to think about these points before taking the next step. In substance, defence, total employment, provision of the basic needs of man and decentralisation are the goals of the economic system envisaged by Jana Sangh."[18]

In substance, it may be said that the thinking of Deendayal was fundamental as well as analytical and integral. He wanted to develop a system which would sustain both the material as well as the spiritual aspects of human life. It may be said that the sum and substance of Deendayal's thinking was to have value-based principles, commitment to values and a social and individual way of life which would preserve the values in life.

REFERENCES

1. Golwalkar, M.S., *Bunch of Thoughts* (Bangalore: Sahitya Sindhu Prakashan), 1966.
2. Kelkar, B.K., *Pandit Deendayal Upadhyaya, Ideology and Perception*, Part III, *Political Thought* (New Delhi: Suruchi Prakashan), 1991, p. 58.
3. *Economic Policy Resolution of Bahratiya Jana Sangh* (Bombay: BJS), April 1964.
4. Kelkar, B.K., *Pandit Deendayal Upadhyaya, Ideology and Perception*, Part III, Political Thought, op. cit., p. 60.
5. Ibid., p. 61.
6. Thuldharia, Badrisha, Daishik Shastra (Pune: Bharatiya Vichar), 1942.
7. *Rashtra Dharma*, July-August 1947.
8. *Panchajanya*, 24 August, 1968.
9. *Rashtra Dharma*, July-August 1947.
10. *Ibid.*, November-December 1950.
11. *Panchajanya*, 13 July, 1959.
12. *Ibid.*, 2 January 1961.
13. *Ibid.*
14. Kelkar, B.K., *Pandit Deendayal Upadhyaya, Ideology and Perception*, Part III, *Political Thought, op. cit.*, p. 69.
15. *Ibid.*
16. *Organiser*, 29 September, 1958.
17. *Ibid.*
18. Bharatiya Jana Sangh Resolutions, 1951-1974.

3

INTEGRAL HUMANISM

Panditji's most valuable contribution is his enunciation of the concept of Integral Humanism. Those deeply involved in the make-and-break politics may mistake Panditji's Integral Humanism as a new 'ism' or doctrine or dogma propounded by him in order to counter all other prevailing isms or to add a new one. It is all too well-known that prophets of an ism or a new political thought claim originality. It is more so in the West. A slight deviation or difference with the current thought entitles a person to proclaim himself founder of a new doctrine. But no such thought ever crossed Panditji's mind. As a true votary of culture, he was not given to this narrowness. He believed in what Lord Krishna said in the *Gita* that true knowledge was timeless. One may observe some variation in its expressed form, owing to varied situations and conditions, but that does not mean the creation of new knowledge. Panditji, through his creative ability and positive outlook put a new gloss on the true and eternal thought current and reinterpreted it to suit the changed and contemporary world. It would be clear, therefore, that Integral Humanism was conceived only to perfect isms so that they could meet the challenges posed to them. It was farthest from his thought to add to the ideological bitterness obtaining in the society by outright rejection or repudiation of any of the contemporary ideas, isms or viewpoints, while expressing his own.[1]

Why This 'Ism' or That

Panditji was opposed to all isms. He only believed that which was truthful and timeless, could face the challenges of change and therefore, could hardly fit into the steel-frame of any ism. In other words, no 'ism' can ever suit all countries and conditions, and for all times. He precisely thought so! But in the modern age people cannot think without an ism and he too adopted the usage only as a compromise for the convenience of his audience.

But to dispel any doubts in this behalf, he used to explain that as one cannot easily concentrate one's mind on *Nirgun* (attributeless) or *Nirakar* (formless) *Brahma,* one needs, in the beginning, to fix one's mind on *Sagun* (of attributes) or *Sakar* (of forms) *Brahma.* Once one gets accustomed to this form of concentration it becomes easier later to do so in respect of the *Nirgun* or *Nirakar Brahma* also. So to grasp easily the real and eternal truth, which is above all isms, first, one has to comprehend fully the reality that exists in this world through the medium of integral humanism.

Seer Not a Philosopher

To engage oneself in constant debate, discourse or a controversy is the function of a philosopher. Panditji was not a philosopher in that sense of the term. To call him so is to belittle him. In the tradition of Indian sages of yore, he was in fact a seer. Therefore, whatever he had seen and perceived, may be called *Darshan.* The word philosophy hardly conveys what Indians mean by the term. This kind of *Darshan* is neither new nor unfamiliar to us. It has flourished in Indian soil.

Every country has its own peculiar historical, social and economic situation, and its leaders decide the remedies for the ills that beset the country from time to time, taking into consideration its background. It is illogical to believe that remedies which the leaders of one country decide to try for their problems are likely to be effective as such to all other peoples. A simple illustration will suffice. Even though the basic organic activity is the same in all human beings, the drugs which may be helpful in England may not prove equally helpful in India. Diseases depend also upon climate, water, dietary habits and heredity. Even though the external symptoms may be apparently similar, the same drug does not necessarily cure all persons. Those who apply a single panacea to all diseases must be considered quacks. rather than doctors. Therefore, Ayurveda states यद्देशेस्य यो जन्तु: तद्देश्य तस्यौषधम् i.e. for the disease in each place, remedy suitable to that place must be found. Therefore, it is neither possible nor wise to adopt foreign isms in our country in the original form *in toto*. It will not be helpful in achieving happiness and prosperity.

Human Knowledge is Common Property

On the other hand, it needs to be realised that not all the thoughts and principles that have sprung up elsewhere are necessarily local in space and time. The response of human beings in a particular place, time and social atmosphere may, and does in many cases, have relation and use to other human beings elsewhere and at other times. Therefore, to ignore altogether the developments in other societies, past or present, is certainly unwise. Whatever truths these developments contain must be taken note of and accepted. The rest must be scrupulously avoided. While absorbing the wisdom of other societies, it is only proper that we avoid their mistakes or perversities. Even their wisdom should be adapted to the particular circumstances. In brief, we must absorb the knowledge and gains of the entire humanity so far as eternal principles and truths are concerned. Of these the ones that originated in our midst have to be clarified and adapted to changed times and those that we take from other societies have to be adapted to our conditions.[2]

The Conflicting Ideals

The western political thought has accepted Nationalism, Democracy and Socialism or Equality as ideals. Besides, now and then, there have been attempts directed at world unity which took the shape of the League of Nations, and after the Second World War, the United Nations Organisation. For a variety of reasons these have not succeeded. However, they were sincere in their attempts in that direction. All these ideals have in practice proved to be incomplete and mutually opposing.

Nationalism led to conflict between nations, which in turn led to global conflict. If *status quo* is regarded as synonymous with world peace, the aspirations of many small nations to be independent would remain ever un-fulfilled. World unity and nationalism conflict with each other. Some advocate suppression of nationalism for world unity, whereas others regard world unity as a utopian ideal and lay emphasis on national interest. Similar difficulty arises in reconciling Socialism and Democracy. Democracy grants individual liberty, but the same is used by capitalist system for exploitation and monopoly. Socialism aimed at putting an end to exploitation but it destroyed freedom and dignity of the individual.

Mankind stands confused, and is unable to decide what the correct path is for future progress. The West is not in a position to say with confidence that "this alone and no other" is the right path. It is itself groping. Therefore, simply to follow the West would be an instance of a blind being led by another.[3]

In this situation, the attention is claimed by the Bharatiya culture. Is it possible that our culture has the answer the world requires?

From the national standpoint, one has to consider the Indian culture because in this very culture nature independence is intimately related to one's own culture. If culture does not form the basis of independence then the political movement for independence would be reduced simply to a scramble by selfish and power-seeking persons. Independence can be meaningful only if it becomes an instrument for the expression of the culture. Such expression will not only contribute to the progress, but the effort required will also give the experience of joy. Therefore, both from the national as well as human standpoint, it has become essential that one thinks of the principles of the Bharatiya culture. If with its help one can reconcile the various ideals of the western political thought, then it will be an added advantage. These western principles are a product of revolution in human thought and social conflict. They represent one or the other aspiration of mankind. Thus, it is not proper to ignore them.

Bharatiya Culture is Integrated

The first characteristic of Bharatiya culture is that it looks upon life as an integrated whole. It has an integrated viewpoint. To think of parts may be proper for a specialist, but it is, not useful from the practical standpoint. The confusion in the West arises primarily from its tendency to think of life in sections and then to attempt to put them together by patch-work. We do admit that there is diversity and plurality in life, but we have always attempted to discover the unity behind them. This attempt is thoroughly scientific. The scientists always attempt to discover order, in the apparent disorder in the universe, to find out the principles governing the universe and frame practical rules on the basis of these principles. Chemists discovered that a few elements comprise the entire physical world. Physicists went one step further and showed that even these elements pulsate with energy. Today we know that the entire universe is only a form of energy.[4]

Philosophers are also basically scientists. The western philosophers reached up to the principle of duality; Hegel put forward the principle of thesis, anti-thesis and synthesis. Karl Marx used this principle as a basis and presented his analysis of history and economics. Darwin considered the principle of survival of the fittest as the sole basis of life. But we, in this country, perceived the basic unity of all life. Even the dualists have believed nature and spirit to be complementary to each other than contradictory. The diversity in life is merely an expression of the internal unity. There is complementarity underlying the diversity. The unity in seed finds expression in various forms—the roots, the trunk, the branches, the leaves, the flowers and the fruits of the tree. All these have different forms and colours and even to some extent different properties. Still we recognise their relation of unity with each other through the seed.

Mutual Conflict—Sign of Cultural Regression

Unity in diversity and the expression of unity in various forms have remained the central thought of Bharatiya culture. If this truth is whole-heartedly accepted then there will not exist any cause for conflict among various powers. Conflict is not a sign of culture or nature; rather it is a symptom of perversion. The law of the jungle, "Survival of the Fittest", which the West discovered in recent years was known to Indian philosophers. Deendayal further elaborated:

"We have recognised desire, anger etc., among the six lower tendencies of human nature, but we did not use them as the foundation or the basis of civilised life or culture. There are thieves and robbers in the society. It is essential to save ourselves and the society from these elements. We cannot consider them as our ideals or standards of human behaviour. Survival of the fittest is the law of the jungle. Civilisations have developed not on the basis of this law but by consideration of how the operation of this law could be reduced to the minimum in human life. If we wish to progress, we have to keep this history of civilisation before our minds."[5]

Mutual Cooperation

Cooperation also obtains in abundance just as conflict and competition in this world. Vegetation and animal life keep each other alive. We get our oxygen supply with the help of vegetation whereas we provide Carbon-dioxide so essential for the growth of vegetable life. This mutual cooperation sustains life on this earth.

The recognition of this element of mutual sustenance among different forms of life and taking that as the basis of an effort to make human life mutually sustaining is the prime characteristic of civilisation. To mould the nature *prakriti* to achieve the social goals is culture *samskriti* but when this nature leads to social conflict, it is perversion *vikriti*. Culture does not disregard or deny nature. Rather it enhances those elements in nature which, are helpful in sustaining life in this universe, and makes it fuller and richer, and curbs others which obstruct or destroy life. Let us take a simple illustration. The relationships such as brother and sister, mother and son, father and son are natural. These are same both in man as well as among animals. Just as two brothers are sons of one mother so also two calves have a single mother cow. Where lies the difference? The animals forget these natural relationships. They cannot build up an edifice of civilisation on these relations. But men use this natural relation as a basis to construct a more harmonious order in life, to establish other relationships flowing from these basic relationships so as to knit the whole society in a single unit of cooperation. Thus various values and traditions are built. Standards of good and bad are determined accordingly. In society we find instances of both affection as well as enmity between brothers. But we consider affection good and aim at enhancing affectionate brotherly relations. The opposite tendency is disapproved. If conflict and enmity are made the basis of human relationships, and if on this basis history is analysed, then it would be futile to dream of a world-peace resulting out of such a course of action.

A mother brings up her children. Mother's love is considered as the highest love. On such a basis alone we can devise the rules regulating the life of mankind. Sometimes, there are examples of selfishness and cruelty of a mother towards her child. Among some species of animals, mother devours her progeny to satisfy her hunger. On the other hand, among monkeys mother carries her child along even after its death. Both types of behaviour are found among living beings. Which of these two principles of nature can be made the basis of civilised life? We cannot but conclude that alone which helps to sustain life can be chosen, the contrary cannot lead to civilised life. Human nature has both tendencies, anger and greed on the one hand and love and sacrifice on the other. All these are present in our nature. Anger, greed, etc. are natural to man and beasts alike. For that reason if we make anger a basis of our life and arrange our efforts accordingly then the result will be a lack of harmony in our life. Therefore, the exhortation, "Do not yield to anger." Even when anger arises in one's mind one can exercise control over it and one should do so. Thus control becomes a standard of our life and not anger.

Such laws are known as the principle of ethics. These principles are not framed by anyone. They are discovered. A suitable analog is that of the law of gravitation. If we throw a stone it falls on the ground. This law of gravitation is not framed by Newton. He discovered it. When he saw an apple falling on the ground from the branch, he realised there must exist such a law. Thus he discovered this law, he did not frame it. Similarly, there are certain principles of human relations. For instance, if one feels anger he must keep it under control. Such an act will be beneficial to all. These principles of ethics are then discovered.

"Do not tell a lie to one another, say what you know to be true". This is a principle. Its usefulness becomes apparent at every step in life. We appreciate a truthful person. If we tell a lie, we ourselves feel unhappy; life cannot go on; there will be great confusion.

These principles constitute our Dharma. A child does not speak untruth by nature. Often parents teach their child to speak untruths. When the child desires something which the parents do not wish to give him, they conceal the object and tell the child that the desired object has disappeared. The child may be befooled for a couple of times, but soon it knows the real situation and learns to speak untruth. The fact that by nature a person is truthful is a law that is discovered. Many other principles of ethics are similarly discovered. They are not arbitrarily framed by someone. In Bharat these principles are termed *Dharma,* laws of life. All those principles which bring about harmony, peace and progress in the life of mankind are included in this term Dharma. On the sound basis of Dharma, then, we must proceed with the analysis of life as an integral whole.

When, nature is channelised according to the principles of Dharma, we have culture and civilisation. It is indeed this culture which will enable us to sustain and sublimate the life of mankind. Dharma is translated here as law. The English word 'religion' is not the correct translation for 'Dharma'.

An integrated life is not only the foundation and the underlying principle of our culture, but also its aim and ideal.

Happiness of an Individual

We have thought of life as integrated not only in the case of collective or social life but also in the individual life. Normally an individual is thought of in the physical bodily form. Physical comfort and luxury are considered happiness. But we know that mental worry destroys bodily happiness. Everyone desires physical comfort. But if a person is imprisoned and there he is given the finest of foods, will he be happy? A person does not experience joy on getting nice food if it is also accompanied by a few abuses. There is a well-known incident in *Mahabharata.* When Lord Krishna went to Hastinapur as an emissary of the Pandavas, Duryodhana invited him to enjoy his hospitality. Lord Krishna declined his invitation and went instead to Vidura's home. Overjoyed by the visit of this much-revered guest, Vidura's wife served the banana skins while throwing away the kernel. But Lord Krishna enjoyed even the meal of banana skin. That is why it is said, "Even a modest meal served with dignity and affection tastes better than the best delicacies served with disrespect." It is necessary, therefore, to take note of the mental happiness.

Similarly, there is an intellectual happiness which too must be considered (Even after a person gets comforts for the body, and prominence, affection, etc., which please the mind, if he is involved in some intellectual confusion he is reduced to a state almost similar to madness). And what is madness itself? A lunatic may have all physical comforts, he may be perfectly healthy and properly cared for by his relatives; but he does not possess intellectual happiness. Intellectual peace is also essential and important. We will have to take al these things into consideration.

The Political Aspirations of Man

Body, mind, intelligence and the soul—these four make up an individual. But these are integrated. We cannot think of each part separately. The confusion that has arisen in the West is due to the fact that they have treated each of the above aspects of human being separately and without any relation to the rest. When there was movement for democratic structure, they proclaimed that "man is a political animal" and therefore, his political aspirations must be attended to. Why only one person should be the king and others his subjects? Let everyone rule. In order to satisfy this political man, they gave him the right to vote. Now he did get the right to a vote, but at the same time other rights diminished. Then the question arose, "The voting right is nice, but what about food? What if there is nothing to eat?"[6]

The reason is that they have not thought of the integrated human being. In our country we have thoroughly considered this matter. That is why we have stated that progress of man means simultaneous progress of the body, mind, intellect and soul of man. Often it has been propagated that Bharatiya Culture thinks only of salvation of the soul, that it does not bother about the rest. This is wrong. We do think of the Soul, but it is not true that we do not consider body, mind and intellect of much importance. Others gave importance to body alone. Therefore, our attention to the soul is unique. With the passage of time, this created an impression that we are concerned only with the soul and not with other aspects of human being. A young unmarried boy cares for his mother, but after marriage he cares both for his wife as well as his mother, and discharges his responsibilities towards both of them. Now if anyone says that this man has no love for his mother, it would be untrue. A wife loves only her husband at first, but after the birth of a child, she loves both, her husband and child. Sometimes an unthoughtful husband feels that his wife neglects him after the birth of their child. But this is generally not correct. If that is true then the wife has certainly dipped in her duty.

Similarly, while we recognise the need to pay attention to the soul, we do not neglect the body. Upanishads declare in unambiguous words: नाडयमात्मा बल हीनेन लम्य: i.e. a weakling cannot be the realist, the Self. Again शरीर माद्यं खलु धर्मसाधनम् or body is truly the primary instrument to discharge the responsibilities of Dharma. The fundamental difference between our position and the West is that, whereas they have regarded body and satisfaction if its desires as the aim, we regard the body as an instrument for achieving our aims. We have recognised the importance of the body only in this light. The satisfaction of our bodily needs is necessary, but we don't consider this to be the sole aim of all our efforts. Here in Bharat we have placed before ourselves the ideal of the fourfold responsibilities of catering to the needs of body, mind, intellect and soul with a view to achieving the integrated progress of man. *Dharma, Artha, Kama* and *Moksha* are the four kinds of *Purushartha*—human efforts. *Purushartha* means, efforts which befit a man. The longings for *Dharma, Artha, Kama* and *Moksha* are in-born in man, and satisfaction of these gives him joy. Of these four efforts too, we have thought in an integrated way. Even though *Moksha* has been considered the highest of these *Purusharthas*, efforts for *Moksha* alone are not considered to bring benefit to the soul. On the other hand, a person who engages in action, while remaining unattached to its fruits, is said to achieve *Moksha* inevitably and earlier.[7]

Artha includes what is known as political and economic policies. According to the ancients, it used to include the Justice and Punishment as well as Economics (*Dandaneeti* and *Vartta*). *Kama* relates to the satisfaction of various natural desires. Dharma includes all those rules, fundamental principles and ethical codes in accordance with which all the activities in respect of *Artha* and *Kama* are to be carried on, and all the goals thereof to be achieved. This alone will ensure progress in an integrated and harmonious manner, and lead ultimately to *Moksha.*

Thus, even though Dharma regulates *Artha* and *Kama*, all the three are interrelated and mutually complementary. Dharma helps achieve *Artha.* Even in business one requires honesty, restraint, truthfulness, etc., which are the attributes of Dharma. Without these qualities one cannot earn money. It must be admitted that Dharma is instrumental in attaining *Artha* and *Kama.* Americans proclaimed, "Honesty is the best business policy". In Europe they said, "Honesty is the best policy." We go one step forward and assert, "Honesty is not a policy but a principle"[8]. We believe in Dharma not just because it is instrumental in acquiring *Artha* but because it is a fundamental principle of civilized life.

Kama too can be attained only through Dharma. Having produced the material things, such as nice food, when, where, how, and in what quantity it will be used, can be determined only by Dharma. If a sick person eats food meant for a healthy one and *vice versa* both of them will be at a disadvantage. Dharma helps in restraining the natural tendencies of man, whereby he is able to determine what is beneficial to him, apart from what is pleasurable. Hence, Dharma is given the foremost place in our culture.

Dharma is of primary importance, but we should not forget that it is not possible to practise Dharma in the absence of *Artha.* There is a saying, "What sin will not be committed by one who is starving? Those who have lost everything become ruthless." Driven by hunger, even a Rishi like Vishwamitra broke into the house of a hunter and ate the flesh of a dog. Therefore, we are enjoined to see that there is enough wealth created continuously, since wealth also strengthens Dharma. Similarly, the government has to maintain law and order and prevent chaos which definitely destroys Dharma. At the time of chaos, the law of the jungle prevails, where the strong feed upon the weak. Therefore, stability in the state is also essential for the prevalence of Dharma. In order to do this, education, character building, spread of idealism and suitable economic structures are all necessary.

Artha is inclusive of political aspects of life as well. Excessive power of the State is also harmful for Dharma. It was said that a king should be neither too harsh nor too soft with his people. Excessive reliance on harsh measures produces a feeling of revolt in people. When the State usurps the rightful place of Dharma, then there is this evil of preponderance of power of the state. Dharma suffers thereby. This is the reason for the decline of Dharma in ruthless States.

When the State acquires all powers, both political and economic, the result is a decline of Dharma. In this way, if the State has unlimited powers, the whole society looks towards the State for everything. Officers of the Government neglect their duties and acquire vested interests. These are all signs of the preponderance of powers of the State, whereby Dharma suffers a setback. Hence *Artha* should not be allowed to acquire on hold in either of these two ways.

Kama too has been considered on the same lines. If the physical needs are neglected, and desires entirely suppressed, Dharma does not grow. Dharma cannot be observed if one has no food to eat. If the fine arts, which satisfy the mind, are altogether stopped, then the civilising influence on people will not be present. Mind will become perverse, and Dharma neglected. On the other hand, if greediness of the gluttons of Rome or sensuousness of Yayati prevails, then duties will be forgotten. Hence Kama too must be pursued in consonance with Dharma.

We have thus considered the life of an individual in a thorough and integrated manner. We have set the aim of developing body, mind, intellect as well as soul in a balanced way. We have tried to satisfy the manifold aspirations of man, taking care that efforts to satisfy two different aspirations are not mutually conflicting. This is the integrated picture of all the fourfold aspirations of an individual. This concept of a complete human being, an integrated individual, is both our goal as well as our path.[9]

Nationalism and Internationalism

What has been said above about man and society relationship is true of nationalism and internationalism. In the West, nationalism is a product of reaction. This is why there has been inherent disharmony between nationalism of two nations and between nationalism and internationalism. We have a nationalistic prayer saying, "I am born in this good nation, give me happiness and glory" *(pradurbhuto surashtre asimin kirtimriddhim dadatu me).* We find more similar prayers for the good of the world. I recall here an occasion during the deliberations of the Vishwa Hindu Sammelan (World Hindu Conference) when a question was posed, 'How to define Hindu?' I cannot deal with the question here in depth but will touch on one aspect: whether Hindu connotes nationalism, internationalism or even something beyond or more. The answer, however, that when the whole world was uncivilized, world civilization invariably was identified with Hindu nationalism.[10] But even in that supreme position we never thought of exploiting other nations in the interests of our own. Our motto was '*Krinvanto, vishwarnaryam*' i.e. we are Aryans and will make the world Aryan—we are cultured and will strive to share our culture and refinement with others and raise their level. This thought forms the base of our positive nationalism, which is a historical fact and which instead of creating clash between nationalism and internationalism provides rudiments of internationalism. We have been averse to the idea that one who claims to be a nationalist cannot be an internationalist and conversely one who is an internationalist cannot be a nationalist. Again the westerners are amazed at it. They fail to grasp how one can be a nationalist and an internationalist both at the same time. But we see no contradiction in it.

Beyond Humanity

What lies next, is beyond the West's comprehension. They, at best, can think of internationalism or humanity and not beyond. But our thought has transgressed this limit and dwells upon still further—the entire life. Only we have conceived life other than human life. There are some among Hindus who feed fish, ants and cows with sugar and flour. Why so? Because they believe all life is like their own. Not only that, even inanimate objects are regarded as part of the creation of the Almighty like their own selves, and worship even stones for they see the Creator in them, as God is immanent. Further, our people inquired of themselves 'what is man?', 'what are other beings?', 'what all this animate, inanimate, sentient, insentient creation is?' and themselves realised later that all creation is one. But they, nevertheless, discovered that unity 'was different from uniformity'. We never believed that all must be uniform but did think that all are one and how strong is this unity has been best expressed in *'Sarvam khalu Idam Brahma'* i.e. all this world is Brahma. Our religion and our country has the capacity to sustain the universe, the creation. Certain principles and ideals are eternal and ever-lasting and therefore immutable. Our religion with the force of these truthful and eternal principles has churned out best thoughts and ideas to suit changing situations and conditions. All apparent contradictions and discord have been harmonised to great extent. If we think of one point or one thing alone, many things appear conflicting. Sometimes we talk of *Karma* (action) and sometimes of *sannyas* (renunciation). On one hand, we believe in *Moksha,* and on the other, in 'all is worthless'. Sometimes we declare *Dharmasya mulam arthah* (money is the root of *Dharma).*[11] But all these apparently different and divergent views have converged into one co-ordinated system which sometimes is unintelligible to an ordinary mind. Relying on Swami Vivekananda, it can be safely said that our religion has the capacity to sustain the society and it has done so for thousands of years. It is true that sufficient thought could not be given to what changes are warranted in the social set up over the last twelve or thirteen hundred years. Again, there is no need to be alarmed at the word 'change' as changes have been effected in the society with the sanction of *Dharma* and philosophy from time to time. It has been said, *Tarkopratishtha shrutayo vibhinna, naiko muniryasya vachah pramanam* i.e. Vedas differ, Smritis differ and words of no Muni should be treated as last word. Unfortunately the lasting peaceful conditions which are required to effect changes eluded us for these twelve or thirteen hundred years and some distortions and flaws crept into the system. Some surgery is undoubtedly needed, but, to quote Gandhiji—'operate the diseased part but do not kill the patient'. Remove the defect but let the system work. Our society is sustaining itself for the last several centuries. We always had ageless and unchanging laws and changing provisions going hand in hand.

Now the question arises, should we accept different western ideologies as progressive, modern and better just because they are new. It would be fair to make a comparative study of the two and take what is best in them. On comparison we find that our *Sanatan Dharma* stands superior to western thought. It has many characteristics but in the present-day context Deendayal had said, "We stand for Integral Humanism".

Modern Dharma

The difference in the two pictures is probably clear now. The principal features of our *Dharma,* as related to contemporary situation, has been termed 'Integral Humanism' by late Panditji. *Sanatan Dharma* more or less has the same make. It is this make which can ensure happiness and prosperity for the mankind through the ages.

A Clear Direction

Now we should also bear in mind that our way of thinking in this country is unique. The reason is that there lies fundamental difference in the basic concepts of Indian philosophy and the thoughts of non-Indian thinkers. Panditji very clearly pointed out that in the According to the Western thinking, various institutions, concepts are compartmentalized. They consider individual, family, society and humanity as separate and non-interacting entities. While dealing with the individual they lost sight of other organs of the society. The same applies to their thinking on family, society and humanity. This is inherent in their contemplation. They confine themselves to one organism. Let us take religion for instance. They have various faiths and sects, but one feature is common to all. Each one believes itself to be only right and others wrong. Now let us look at our own country. We too have numerous faiths and beliefs but here we say, "My path is right and so is yours". The West asserts, "My religion alone leads to God!" This is the western metaphysics while India says, "Your religion also leads to God." The same approach is found in socio-economic matters. They have concentrated on one entity as if it has no correlation or interaction with the other. For the sake of clearer understanding one would add that in their system the individual forms the centre and around it are concentric circles representing family, community, nation, and humanity respectively.

This is concentric arrangement in which individual is the centre. The circles though surrounded the centre, yet have no interdependent existence and each has its separate function, without interplay. Against this, our arrangement, which is not new but ancient, is an ever expanding spiral. It begins with the individual but goes on enlarging: individual to family, family to society, society to nation, nation to humanity and ultimately to the universe or *Srishti* without ever delinking with the Centre, i.e. the individual.

Difference

The difference of the two systems is worthy of note. We dwelt upon the individual, family, community, society, nation and mankind. And so did they. But these two systems widely differ. They treated all as distinct, though concentric entities, with no inter-relationship, but we did not. So their thought remained exclusive.

In Indian system, on the other hand, one entity originates from the other and expands into the next, thus forming an infinite spiral with no inner conflicts and no tensions. Individual nowhere comes into clash with family, on family with community, and so on. Not only that one is not opposed to the other, we have gone a step further, as we believe one is complementary to the other. To further illustrate the point: An infant knows little about anything but himself. His world is confined to his ownself: As he grows, he recognises his parents, his brothers, sisters and the people around him, and thus develops the awareness of family, but this awareness does not negate his 'I'. To him 'I' and the 'family' both are a reality. He grows and develops his mind and becomes capable of action. He then forms a community with people of like mind and like action and becomes indistinguishable and inseparable from his community. By and by he develops an identity with the nation and becomes one

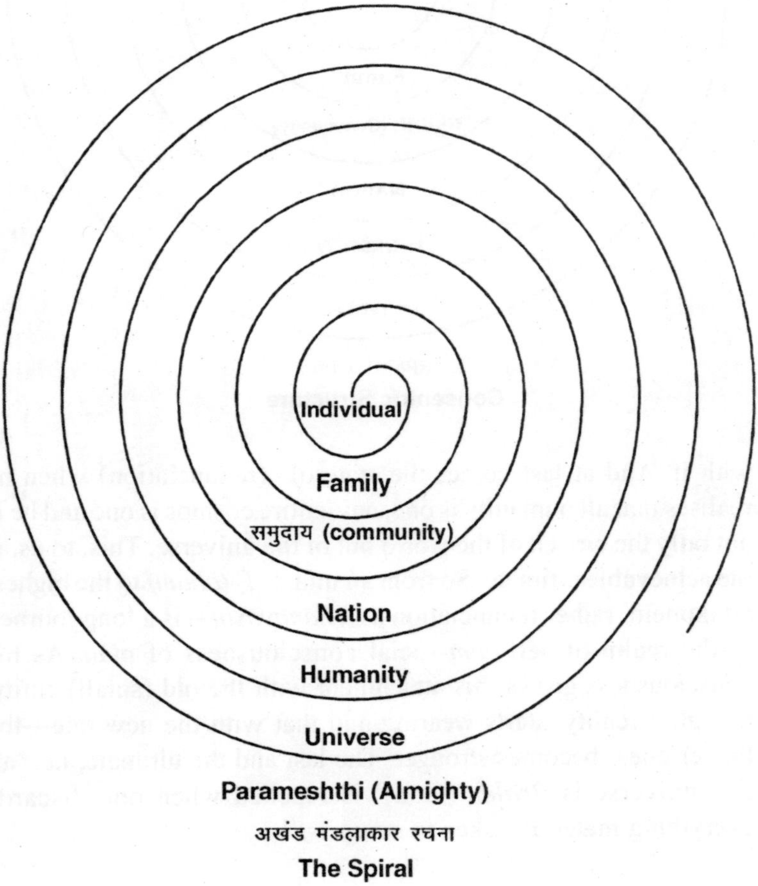

अखंड मंडलाकार रचना
The Spiral

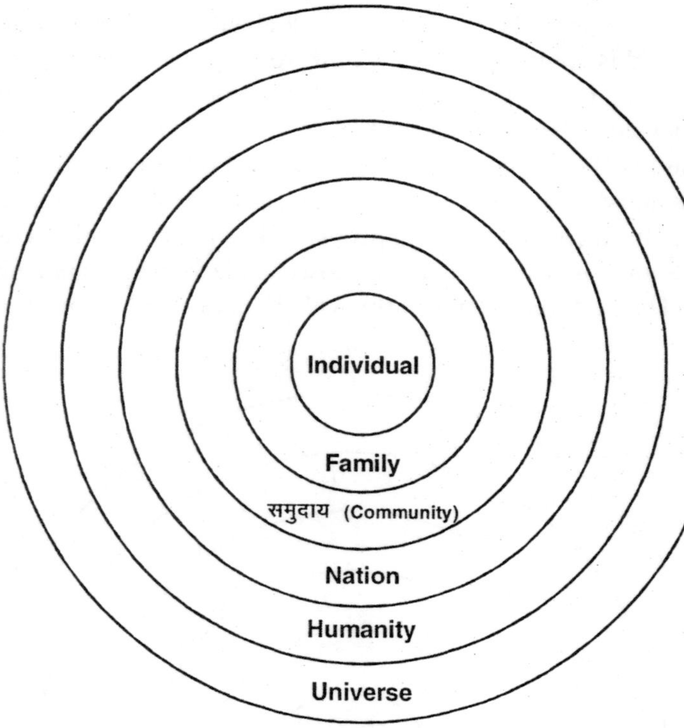

संकेन्द्री रचना

Concentric Structure

with it. And at last comes the state of (renunciation) when he realises that all humanity is one, nay, entire cosmos is one and he is not only the citizen of the world but of the universe. This, to us, is the achievable ultimate. So from an infant *'I' (aham)* to the highest attainment, rather renunciation as a *Sannyasin*—is a long journey in the realm of self-*cum*-social consciousness of man. As his consciousness grows, his attachment with the old (small) entity, though a reality, starts wearing and that with the new one—the bigger one—becomes stronger. The last and the ultimate, i.e. 'all this universe is *Brahm* (God)' is reached when one discards everything material (takes to *sannyas)*[13].

No Chaos

In other words, all units or entities are realities of life. As our consciousness grows, our vision widens. As all are realities, one is not at cross purpose with the other. None can be denied and none discarded. This is like the seed sprouting into plant, plant growing into a tree and the tree blossoming and bearing the fruits. The seed, the plant, the flowers and the fruit, all look different. None appears to have any relation with the other. To some, it may appear that there is a chaos in the nature. But is it so? Not at all. All this is the process of evolution, growth and development. There is no conflict between the seed and the tree. The tiniest and the tallest entities, though have their independent existence, together form a single, integrated whole. Indian way of thinking is akin to this.

Why Integrated Life

We have laid enough emphasis on individual, the smallest unit, and rightly so. We conceive of an individual so organised and integrated, as is unknown to the West. There the stress is on material progress. As you know, the USA is considered to be the most advanced nation and country. They have attained a high level of prosperity but is not it surprising that common people there should be deprived of happiness and contentment. Their life seems plagued with contradictions, strife, unrest, highest crime incidence, suicides etc. It has led to high blood pressure, heart ailments and criminal tendencies. The country which has the capacity to buy the whole world has been unable to buy mental peace. So we are constrained to think, 'What, after all is our goal? It is happiness which is enduring and real. Europe in spite of limitless acquisition is groping for happiness. Christ rightly said that even if an individule has the whole world and yet loses his soul he is the loser. The West has reached the moon but has lost its happiness. On the contrary, our smallest unit, the individual is more organised and integrated. He is not divided or torn. An American psychologist has said of American society, 'Our roads are full of crowds of isolated, solitary and self-alienated humans'. When they are so isolated within themselves, what use they can be of to the world? There is no harmony between the individual and the society. The ill lies in considering man a physical and economic being. They think that once man is given money and material comfort, happiness and peace will follow. But this expectation is belied. This is why highest standards of living failed to bring in its wake the much sought after happiness. This flows from the defect that they always thought in isolation, in bits, so to say, and never thought of various facets of human nature and its needs, except that man is an economic being.

Limited

We admit that man is also an economic being and let there be no doubt about it. His needs of food, sleep, fear and sex *(aahar, nidra, bhaya, maithunam cha)* must be satisfied. But this was not enough and we did not stop here. We thought that man was something more than economic being. He is a physical, psychological, political, social and religious being too. As I have said, his individuality has many facets. Therefore, if all aspects of human nature are not attended to in entirety he will be deprived of the state of real happiness and contentment. In our wholesome thinking while we did not neglect man's needs and desires and conceded that they should be satisfied, we also imposed reasonable restraints. It is not true that only Freud gave serious thought to sex. In this country, sex has been treated in all seriousness, an indispensable force. In the *Gita* it has been said:[14]

> इन्द्रियाणि पराण्या हुरिन्द्रियभ्यः परं मन।
> मनसस्तु पराबुद्धिर्यो बुद्धेः परतस्तु सः।।

It means senses are above desires, mind is above senses, intellect is above mind and soul (*atman*); it is indescribable and above all. Some scholars have interpreted this *shloka* as *Kama*, the sexual desire. But even if this is agreed, sex has not been left unbridled and unrestrained. It has been subjected to restrictions. Lord Krishna himself claims, "I am *Kama*", but at the same time he also says, "*Kama* should be satisfied but not against *Dharma*."[15]

Life Based on Dharma

Like sex, we admit, money has a place in life. Man should be able to satisfy his material needs. One need not have to worry night and day about how to fill his belly. He should have enough leisure to devote it to literary, artistic and cultural pursuits, and also to God, if he so desires. Thus, while taking full cognisance of money and sex, man has been cautioned against their use beyond a reasonable limit, lest it may spell his doom and disintegrate the society. Our ancient seers were very conscious of the possible pitfalls and evolved a philosophy which incorporated some *eternal* and some *universal* laws. They did not merely search, codify or compile such laws. They also perceived and tested them. The sum total of the perceived laws—eternal and universal—made to prevent the individual from falling, the society from degeneration and, for the highest development and progress of the individual is known as *Dharma.* But *Dharma* alone is not enough. Money and sex were not ignored. They were, however, sandwiched between *Dharma* on one end, and *Moksha,* the salvation, on the other. Thus was evolved a quartet of *Dharma, Artha, Kama* and *Moksha* for guiding the human endeavour and enterprise. This being a co-ordinated, organised and integrated system did not divide or split the individual and gave him full and free choice of his life's goals and ideals, best suited to his physical, mental, intellectual and spiritual capacities and capabilities, keeping his individuality intact.

The Central Idea of PIH

The Central idea of PIH is that while humanity and the entire animate and inanimate nature around man are full of almost infinite diversity, it all has got a common *Atma* (nearest English rendering is Ethos or Soul). The diversity is superficial, and because of the common *Atma,* all are cooperative and complementary. This is expressed by the word *Ekatmata*.

Man is a conglomerate of body, mind, intellect and Soul. Therefore, we must think of the well-being and development of all these four consistently with the well-being and progress of the society. Along with the material development, we have to consider the moral and spiritual development also. With all this in view, Bharatiya culture has placed four objectives before every individual. Those objectives are called the *Purusharthas.*

The four *Purusharthas* (objectives) are *Dharma* (moral duties and divine laws), *Artha* (wealth), *Kama* (desires) and *Moksha* (complete liberation and salvation). Everybody has the set objectives in mind. But it will be wrong either to assume anyone of these as the sole inspiration for any man, or to assume success in it as the only measure of a man's success in life. Bharatiya culture considers all these as essential. Only when *Artha* and *Kama* are secured according to rules laid down by *Dharma,* the achievement gives happiness to the individual and benefits the society.

The individual personality made of body, mind, intellect and soul is, however, not confined to 'I' only but is related to other people around him. And so the society has also to be considered along with the individual.

Society also has its body, mind, intellect and soul and it also has its four *Purusharthas* (objectives) in its life. But since the individual and the society are *Ekatma,* there is no conflict in their interests; they are mutually complementary.

For the attainment of the *Purusharthas*, a number of institutions and systems are created. An individual is involved in more than one of these, i.e. an individual's personality is multifaceted. Only when an individual thinks and acts in the awareness that he and the society are *Ekatma,* will his actions be conducive to common good.

Any system in which an individual is considered only as a part of a large heartless machine, or at the other extreme regards an individual as a self-centred man who does not care for the society, is a defective system. Similarly, any system which takes into account only one or two out of the four (body-mind-intellect-soul) needs of man, is also an imperfect system.

The ideal man according to this philosophy is he who takes a view of human life based on the four *Purusharthas* and works for them; not only this but he looks further beyond the family and the nation right upto the world human community, nay he even goes further and encompasses the whole nature and its maker. If we consider various aspects of life and the systems or arrangements, while constructing a plan to guide human outlook and action, there will be rapid progress in equality, nationality, philanthrophy and world peace; the internal tussle and contradictions met with at present in the attempts of achieving these ideals will vanish and their place will be taken by co-operation and compatibility.[16]

REFERENCES

1. Golwalkar, M.S., *Deendayal Upadhyaya and D.B. Thingadi, Integral Approach* (New Delhi: Suruchi Prakashan), 1991, pp. 85-86.
2. *Ibid.*, p. 18.
3. Nene, V.V., *Pandit Deendayal Upadhyaya, Ideology and Perception*, Part II. *Integral Humanism* (New Delhi: Suruchi Prakashan), 1991, p. 27.
4. Golwalkar, M.S., *Deendayal Upadhyaya and D.B. Thingadi, Integral Approach, op. cit.*, p. 20.
5. *Ibid.*, p. 21.
6. *Ibid.*, p. 26.
7. Nene, V.V., *Pandit Deendayal Upadhyaya, Ideology and Perception*, Part II, *Integral Humanism, op. cit.*, p. 41.
8. Golwalkar, M.S., *Deendayal Upadhyaya and D.B. Thingadi, Integral Approach, op. cit.*, p. 20.
9. *Organiser*, 23 April 1965.
10. *Ibid.*
11. *Panchajanya*, 24 August 1968.
12. Golwalkar, M.S., *Deendayal Upadhyaya and D.B. Thingadi, Integral Approach, op. cit.*, p. 102.
13. *Ibid.*, p. 105.
14. *The Gita* 3-42.
15. Golwalkar, M.S., *Deendayal Upadhyaya and D.B. Thingadi, Integral Approach, op. cit.*, pp. 107-108.
16. Nene, V.V., *Pandit Deendayal Upadhyaya, Ideology and Perception, Part II, Integral Humanism, op. cit.*, pp. 11-13.

4

INDIVIDUAL AND COLLECTIVITY

Man is an individual. There are different aspects of an individual's personality, different levels of needs for an individual. In order to develop complete personality, to satisfy the needs progressively and simultaneously at all levels, certain specific kinds of efforts *purusharthas* are needed. But man does not exist merely as an individual. An individual comprising body, mind, intellect and soul is not only a singular 'I', but is also inseparably related to the plural 'We'. Therefore, we must also think of the group or the society.

It is a simple truth that society is group of men. But how did society come into being? Many views have been put forward by philosophers. Those propounded in the West and on which the Western socio-political structure is based describes society as a group of individuals who having entered into an agreement among themselves, brought it into being, This view is known as the "Social Contract Theory". According to this theory individual is given greater importance. If there are any differences in different western views, these pertain only to the questions, namely, "If the individuals produced a society, then in whom, the residual power remains vested, in the society or in the individual? Does the individual have the right to change the society? Can the society impose a variety of regulations on the individual and claim a right to the allegiance of the individual to itself? Or is the individual free in regard to these questions?"[1]

Individual *Versus* Society

There is a controversy in the West on this question. Some have advocated the supremacy of the society and from this a conflict has arisen. The view that individuals have brought the society into being is fundamentally incorrect. It is true that the society is composed of a number of individuals. Yet it is not created by the individuals, nor does it come into being by mere coming together of a number of individuals.

Actually society is self-born. Like an individual, society comes into existence in an organic way. People do not produce society. It is not a sort of club or some joint-stock company, or a registered cooperative society. In reality, society is an entity with its own 'self', its own life; it is a sovereign being like an individual; it is an organic entity. The view that society is an arbitrary association cannot be accepted. It has its own life. Society too has its body, mind, intellect and soul. Some western psychologists are beginning to accept this truth. William McDougal has propounded a new branch of psychology which deals with "group mind". He has accepted that the group has its own mind, its own psychology, its own methods of thinking and action.[2]

Group has its feelings too. These are not exactly similar to the individual's feelings. Group feelings cannot be considered a mere arithmetical addition of individual feelings. Group strength too is not a mere sum of individuals' strength. The intellect, emotions, energies and strength of a group are fundamentally different from those of an individual. Therefore, at times it is experienced that even a weakling, despite his individual weak physique, turns out to be a heroic member of the society. Sometimes an individual may be ready to put up with an affront to his personal self, but is unwilling to tolerate an insult to his society. A person may be ready to forgive and forget a personal abuse to him, but, the same loses his temper if you abuse his society. It is possible that a person who is of a high character in his personal life is unscrupulous as a member of the society. Similarly, an individual can be good in his social life, but cannot be so in his personal life. This is a very important point.

If this situation is analysed, it becomes clear that the modes of thinking of an individual and of a society are not always the same. These two do not bear an arithmetical relation. If a thousand men gather together, it cannot be said for certain that they will think similarly of good things.

Why Mighty Nations of Antiquity Perished

It is known that some ancient nations disappeared. The ancient Greek nation came to an end. Similarly, Egyptian civilisation disappeared. Babilonian and Syrian civilisations are a matter of history. Cynthians perished. Was there ever a time when the citizens of those nations stopped living together? The fact is that there were wide differences among the people that led to the downfall of these nations.

Greece in the past produced Alexander and Herodotus, Ulysses and Aristotle, Socrates and Plato, and the present-day Greece is inhabited by people of the same hereditary stock. There was no interruption in their heredity, because there never was a time when the whole of Greece was devoid of human population and when a new race inhabited that country. Such a thing never happened. Father and son tradition of old Greece was never interrupted. It is possible to trace the ancestry of present-day Greeks to the old Greeks, some 250 to 500 generations back. Despite all this, the old Greek nation is non-existent. So also the old Egyptian nation is no longer there. New nations have risen in those places. How did this happen? This simple fact is indisputable that nations do not come into existence by a mere co-habitation. There was never a time in the lives of the citizens of these decadent nations, when they stopped living in a group. On the other hand, Israeli Jews lived for centuries with other peoples scattered far and wide, yet they did not lose their identity in the societies in which they lived. It is clear, therefore, that the source of national feeling is not in staying on a particular piece of land, but in something else.[3]

What is a Nation?

That source is in the goal which is put before the people. When a group of persons lives with a goal, an ideal, a mission, and looks upon a particular piece of land as motherland, this group constitutes a nation. If either of the two—an ideal and a motherland—is not there, then there is no nation. There is a "Self" in the body, the essence of the individual; upon the severance of its relation with the body, a person is said to die. Similarly, there is this idea, ideal, or fundamental principle of a nation, its soul. Although, it is believed that man takes birth again and again, yet the reborn person is a different individual. They are treated as two separate beings. The same soul leaves one body and enters another, but the previous and the latter are two different individuals. The end of a person is nothing but the departure of his soul from his body. The other components of the body also undergo change. From childhood to old age, there is a drastic change! The biologists tell us that in the course of a few years, every cell of our body is replaced by a new one. A variety of changes takes place. Because the soul resides in the body without interruption, the body continues its existence. Such a relation is known as "The Law of Identity" in logic. It is due to this identity that we admit the continuity of any entity. In this connection a nice illustration of a barber's razor is sometimes advanced.

Once while shaving a customer, a barber prided in his razor being 60 years old. His father too had worked with the same razor. The customer was surprised, especially because the handle was quite, shiny and new in appearance. "Why the handle is so shiny? How have you preserved the brightness for sixty years?" he asked. The Barber was amused with this and replied: "Is it possible to preserve the handle in a brand-new appearance for sixty years? It has been replaced only six months ago". The customer was curious, "And how old is the blade?" "Three years", was the reply. In brief, the handle was replaced, the blade was also replaced, but the razor remained old! Its identity was intact. Similarly, a nation too has a soul. There is a technical name fix for it. In the "Principles and Policies" adopted by Deendayal, the word *Chiti* is mentioned. According to McDougal, every group of persons has an innate nature, which is in-born, and is not the result of historical circumstances.

A human being is born with a soul. Human personality, soul, and character are all distinct from one another. Personality results from a cumulative effect of all the actions, thoughts and impressions of an individual. But soul is unaffected by this history. Similarly, national culture is continuously modified and enlarged by the historic reasons and circumstances. Culture, does include all they things which, by the association, endeavours, and the history of the society, have come to be held as good and commendable, but they are not added on to Chiti. Chiti is fundamental and is central to the nation from its very beginning. Chiti determines the direction in which the nation is to advance culturally. Whatever is in accordance with Chiti is included in culture.[4]

Chiti - Culture - *Dharma*

By way of an illustration, consider the story of *Mahabharata*. The Kauravas were defeated and the Pandavas won. Why did we hold the conduct of the Pandavas as Dharma? Or Why was this battle not considered just a battle for a kingdom? The praise for Yudhishthira and the dishonour heaped on Duryodhana are not a result of political causes. Krishna killed his maternal uncle Kansa, the established king of the times. Instead of branding this as a revolt, we consider Krishna as an *avatar* of God, and Kansa as an *asura*.

Rama was assisted in his invasion of Lanka by Vibhishana, brother of Ravana. Such conduct of Vibhishana, instead of being branded as treason, is considered good and exemplary. He betrayed his brother and his king, even as Jaichand had done later on. He might be branded as a "quisling". But Vibhishana is not called "quisling" by anyone. On the contrary, he is highly praised for his conduct, and Ravana's actions are disapproved. Why is it so? The reason behind this is not political.

If there is any standard for determining the merits and demerits of a particular action, it is this *Chiti*: whatever is in accordance with our nature or *Chiti* is approved and added on to culture. These things are to be cultivated. Whatever is against is discarded as perversion, undesirable, and is to be avoided. *Chiti* is the touch-stone on which each action, each attitude is and tested, and determined to be acceptable or otherwise. *Chiti* is the soul of the nation. It is on the foundation of this *Chiti* (soul) that nation arises and becomes strong and virile. And it is this *Chiti* that is manifested in the actions of every great man of a nation.[5]

An individual is also an instrument in bringing forth the soul of the nation—Chiti. Thus, apart from his own self, an individual also represents his nation. Not only that, he also manns the various institutions that are created for the fulfilment of the national goal. Therefore, he represents these too. The groups larger than nation, such as 'mankind', are also represented by him. In short, an individual has a multitude of aspects, they are not conflicting; there is cooperation, unity and harmony in them. A system based on the recognition of this mutually complementary nature of the different ideals of mankind, their essential harmony, a system which devises laws, which removes disharmony and enhances their mutual usefulness and cooperation, alone can bring peace and happiness to mankind, and can ensure steady development.

"Institution"—A Means to Fulfil National Needs

According to Darwin's theory, living beings develop various organs as per the requirements dictated by the circumstances. In the *shastras*, it was stated slightly differently, that the soul constructs, using the strength of *Prana*, various organs as the need is felt for the purpose of continuing life. Just as the soul produced these different organs in the body, so also in the nation many different organs are produced as instruments to achieve national goals. Like various departments in a factory, such as buildings, machinery, sales, production, maintenance etc., nations also produce different departments, which are called institutions. These institutions are created to fulfil the needs of a nation. Family, castes, guilds (which are now known as trade unions) etc. are such institutions. Property and marriage are also institutions. Formerly there were no marriages. Later on some Rishi established this practice of marriage. Similarly, *Gurukul* and *Rishikul* were institutions. In the same way, the state is also an institution. The nation creates it. A lot of trouble in the West is due to the fact that they confused the state with the nation, they considered the state synonymous with the nation. Truly speaking, nation and state are not the same. In our country, the state was produced as per the social contract theory. Formerly, there was no king. *Mahabharata* describes that in Kritayuga, there was no state, or king. Society was sustained and protected mutually by practising *Dharma*.

Later on, interruption and disorganisation came into existence. Greed and anger dominated. Dharma was on the decline, and the rule of "might is right" prevailed. The Rishis were perturbed over the developments. They all went to Brahma to seek counsel. Brahma gave them a treatise on "Law and the Functions of the State", which he had himself written. At the same time he asked Manu to become the first king. Manu declined saying that a king will have to punish other persons, put them in jail and so on; he was not prepared to commit all these sins. Thereupon Brahma said, "Your actions in the capacity of a king will not constitute sin, as long as they are aimed at securing conditions under which the society can live peacefully and according to Dharma. This will be your duty, your Dharma. Not only that but you will also have a share of the Karma of your subjects, whereby you will gain Dharma considerably if your subjects maintain conduct according to Dharma".[6] Although it is not explicitly stated here, if the society under any king committed sin, a part of that too must automatically go to the account of the king. It is not proper if only good things are shared by the king and not the bad ones; both must be shared in the same proportion. Thus the state came into existence as a contract. This contract theory can be applied to the state, but not to the nation. In the West, it was exactly opposite. Society as a nation, according to them, was a contract, but the king claimed a divine right and proclaimed himself the sole representative of God. This is wrong. In our country, the king may have been first recognised in antiquity but the society as a nation is considered self-born. The state is only an institution.

Similarly, other institutions, like the state, are created from time to time as the need is felt. Every individual is a limb of one or more of these institutions. A person is a member of his family as well as his community; he may also be a member of some association of his fellow professionals, if he pursues a profession. Above all, he is a member of the nation and society. If we consider even the larger sphere, he is a member of the whole mankind, and then the entire universe. Truly speaking, an individual is not merely a single entity, but a plural entity. He is a part of not just one, but a member of many institutions. He lives a variety of lives. The most important aspect is that, despite this multiple personality, he can and should behave in a way which does not bring different aspects of his life into mutual conflict, but which is mutually sustaining, complementary and unifying. This quality is inherent in man.

A person who uses this quality properly, becomes happy. On the other hand, one who does not do so reaps unhappiness. Such a person will not have balanced development in life. As illustration, a man is son of his mother, husband of his wife, brother of his sister and father of his son. A single individual is a father and is also a son, he is a brother and also a husband. He has to maintain all these relations with intelligence, understanding and tact. Where a person fails to do so, there is conflict. If he sides with one party, the other feels wronged. The conflict between his wife and his sister, his wife and mother, result from his inability to behave properly. Thereupon some of his relations are strained. He is pained because his duties towards his mother and towards his wife clash. When he can resolve this conflict, and fulfil all his obligations properly, it can be said that his development will be integrated.

Society and Individual not Conflicting

We do not accept the view that there is any permanent inevitable conflict among the multi-dimentional personality of an individual and different institutions of the society. If a conflict does exist, it is a sign of decadence, perversion and not of nature or culture. The error in Western thinking lies in the fact that some people there believe that human progress is result of this fundamental conflict. Therefore, they consider the conflict between the individual and the state as a natural occurrence, and on the same basis they also theorised on the class-conflict.

Classes do exist in a society. Here too, there were castes, but there was no accepted conflict between one caste and another as a fundamental concept underlying it. The four castes were thought of as analogous to the different limbs of *Virat-Purusha*. It was suggested that the Brahmins were created from the head of the *Virat-Purusha*, the *Kshatriyas* from his hands, the *Vaishyas* from his abdomen and the *Shudras* from his legs. While analysing this concept we are faced with the question whether there can arise any conflict among the head, arms, stomach and legs of the same *Virat-Purusha*. If conflict is fundamental, the body cannot be maintained. The body cannot be maintained if there is any conflict in the different parts of the same body. On the contrary, "one man" prevails. These limbs are not only complementary to one another, but also have their own individuality, unity. There is a complete identity of interest, identity of belonging (The origin of the caste system was on the above basis). If this idea is not kept alive, the castes, instead of being complementary, can produce conflict. But then this is a distortion. It is not a systematic arrangement. Rather, there is a lack of any plan or arrangement. This is indeed the present condition of our society.[7]

This process of deterioration can set in the various institutions of a society, due to a variety of reasons. If the soul of the society weakens, then all the different limbs of the society will grow feeble and ineffective. Any particular institution may be rendered useless or even harmful. Besides, the need and the usefulness of any particular institution may change with time, place and circumstances. While examining the present state of an institution, we also need to think of what it should be like. Mutual complementarity and a sense of unity alone can be the standards of proper conduct. Family, Community, Trade Union, Gram Panchayat, Janapada, State and such other institutions are various limbs of the nation and even of mankind. They are interdependent, mutually complementary. There should be a sense of unity through all of them. For this very reason, there should be a tendency towards mutual accommodation in them, instead of conflict or opposition.

The state is one of the several institutions, an important one, but is not above all others. One of the major reasons for the problems of the present-day world is that almost every one thinks of the state to be synonymous with the society. At least in practice, they consider the state as the sole representative of the society. Other institutions have declined in their effectiveness while the state has become dominant to such an extent that all the powers are gradually being centralised in the state.

The state was not considered the sole representative of the nation. Our national life continued uninterruptedly even after the state went in the hands of foreigners. The Persian nation came to an end with their loss of independence. In our country, there were foreign rules now and then in various parts of the country. At some point of time the Pathans seized the throne of Delhi, and then the Turks, the Mughals, and the British too established their rules. Despite all this, our national life went on, because the state was not its centre. If we had considered state as the centre, we would have been finished as a nation long time ago. In some tales for children it is described that an evil spirit resided in some parrot, and to kill the evil spirit one had to kill the parrot. Those nations whose life centred in the state were finished with the end of the state. On the other hand, where state was not believed central to its life, the nation survived the transfer of political power.

This had its bad effects also. Dr. B.R. Ambedkar had said that our Gram Panchayats were so strong that we neglected the throne of Delhi. We did not remain alert as regards the state as much as we ought to have done, thinking that nation's life did not depend on the state. We forgot that, though it may not be central, the state is definitely an important institution serving some needs of the nation like a limb of the body. It is possible to pluck a hair without much harm, but along with the hair if some skin is also removed, and a little further, if the head too is cut off, then there will be great loss for the body. Therefore, the body must be protected. Although the various limbs of the body are not absolutely indispensable, yet each of them serves an important purpose. From the same standpoint, state too should have been deemed important in the life of a nation. There were persons who had paid attention to this aspect. It was for this reason that the great teacher of Shivaji, Samarth Ramdas Swami, directed him to establish his kingdom. Dharma wields its own power. Dharma is important in life. Shri Ramdas would as well have preached to Shivaji to become a mendicant and spread Dharma following his own example. But on the contrary, he inspired Shivaji to extend his rule, because state too is an important institution of the society. However, to consider something important is different from saying that it is supreme. The state is not supreme. The question arises, then, that if the state is not of fundamental importance, what is it that is absolutely important? Let us consider this question.[8]

Dharma Sustains the Society

We shall have to examine the reasons why the sate was established. No one will dispute that the state must have some specific aim, some ideal. Then this aim or ideal must be considered of highest importance rather than the state which is created to fulfil this ideal. As a watchman is not deemed greater than the treasure he is supposed to protect, so is the case with the treasurer. The state is brought into existence to protect the nation, and to produce right conditions in which the ideals of the nation can be translated into reality. The ideals of the nation constitute *Chiti*, which is analogous to the soul of an individual. It requires some effort to comprehend *Chiti*. The laws that help manifest and maintain *Chiti* of a Nation are termed Dharma of that nation. Hence it is this 'Dharrna' that is supreme. Dharma is the repository of the nation's soul. If Dharma is destroyed, the nation perishes. Anyone who abandons Dharma, betrays the nation.

Dharma is not confined to temples or mosques. Worship of God is only a part of Dharma. Dharma is much wider. In the past, temples have served as effective medium to educate people in their Dharma. However, just as schools themselves do not constitute knowledge, so also temples do not constitute Dharma. A child may attend school regularly and yet may remain uneducated. So also, it is possible that a person may visit temple or mosque without break and yet he may not know his Dharma. To attend temple or mosque constitutes a part of religion, sect, creed, but not necessarily Dharma. Many misconceptions have originated from faulty English translations, and the one most harmful of them is due to the confusion of Dharma with religion.

Dharma and Religion are Different

On the one hand, we used the word religion as synonymous with Dharma, and on the other hand, increasing ignorance, neglect of our society and Dharma, and greater acceptance of European life became the outstanding features of our education. As a result, all the characteristics of a narrow religion, especially as practiced in the West, were attributed automatically to the concept of Dharma also. Since in the West, injustice, atrocities, were perpetrated, bitter conflicts and battles were fought in the name of religion, all these were *en bloc* listed on the debit side of Dharma also. We felt that in the name of Dharma also battles were fought. However, battles of religion and battles for Dharma are two different things. Religion means a creed, or a sect; it does not mean Dharma. Dharma is a very wide concept. It is concerned with all aspects of life. It sustains the society. Even further, it sustains the whole world. That which sustains is *Dharma*.

The fundamental principles of Dharma are eternal and universal. Yet, their implementation may differ according to time, place and circumstance. It is a fact that a human being requires food for maintaining his body. However, what a particular person should eat, in how much quantity, at what intervals, all these are decided according to circumstances. It is possible at times that even fasting is advisable. If a typhoid patient is given normal food, the consequences may be disastrous. For such a person, keeping away from food is necessary. Similarly, the principles of Dharma have to be adapted to changing times and place.[9]

If we carry this concept of Dharma even further, not only the State and the Nation, but the nature of the entire mankind will have to be considered. In other words, the constitution of a nation cannot be contrary to the natural laws. There are a number of norms of behaviour which are not found in any statute book, yet they do exist. At times they are even stronger and more binding than any statutory law. The precept that one should respect one's parents is not written in any law. The present day governments which are turning out variety of laws, day in and day out, have not passed a law to this effect. Still, people respect their parents. Those who do not are criticized. If tomorrow there arises a discussion, even in a court, it will be generally accepted that as long as a person does not attain majority, he should accept his parents' decisions.

Thus the fundamental law of human nature is the standard for deciding the propriety of behaviour in various situations. We have termed this very law as 'Dharma'. The nearest equivalent English term for Dharma can be "Innate law", which, however, does not express the full meaning of Dharma. Since 'Dharma' is supreme, our ideal of the State has been "Dharma-Rajya". The king is supposed to protect Dharma. In olden times at the coronation ceremony the king used to recite three times: "There is no authority which can punish me" (Similar claim was made by kings in the western countries, i.e., it was said, "King can do no wrong", and hence nobody could punish the king). Upon this, the Purohit used to strike the king on his back with a staff saying, "No, you are subject to the rule of Dharma. You are not sovereign." The king used to run around the sacred fire and the Purohit would follow him striking him with the staff. Thus after completing three rounds, ceremony would come to an end. Thereby the king was unambiguously told that he was not an unpunishable sovereign. Dharma was above him.[10] That is, even he was subject to Dharma. Can the people do whatever they please? It may be contended that democracy means just that. The people can do what they please. But in our country, even if people wish, they are not free to act wary to Dharma. Once a priest was asked: "If God is omnipotent, can he act contrary to Dharma? If He cannot, he is not omnipotent." This was a dilemma. Can God practice *adharma*, or is he not omnipotent? Actually God cannot act contrary to Dharma. If he does, then he is not omnipotent. Adharma is a characteristic of weakness, not of strength. If fire, instead of emitting heat, dies out, it is no longer strong. Strength lies not in unrestrained behaviour, but in well-regulated action. Therefore, God who is omnipotent is also self-regulated and consequently fully in tune with Dharma. God descends in human body to destroy Adharma and re-establish Dharma, not to act on passing whims and fancies. Hence even God who can do everything cannot act contrary to Dharma. But, at the risk of being misunderstood, one can say that Dharma is even greater than God. The universe is sustained because He acts according to Dharma. The king was supposed to be a symbol of Vishnu, inasmuch as he was the chief protector of *Dharma-Rajya*.[11]

Dharma-Rajya does not mean a theocratic State. Let us be very clear on this point. Where a particular sect and its prophets or guru rule supreme, that is a theocratic State. All the rights are enjoyed by the followers of this particular sect. Others either cannot live in that country or at best enjoy a slave like, secondary-citizen's status. Holy Roman Empire had this basis. The same concept was existing behind "Khilafat". The Muslim kings world-over used to rule in the name of Khalifa. After the First World War, this came to an end. Now efforts are afoot to revive it. Pakistan is the most recent theocratic State. They call themselves an Islamic State. There, apart from Muslims, all the rest are second-class citizens. This does not happen in a Dharma-Rajya. Rather there is freedom to worship according to one's own religion. In a theocratic State one religion has all the rights and advantages, and there are direct or indirect restrictions on all other religions.[12] *Dharma-Rajya* accepts the importance of religion for peace, happiness and progress of an individual. Therefore, the State has the responsibility to maintain an atmosphere in which every individual can follow the religion of his choice and live in peace. The freedom to follow one's own religion necessarily requires tolerance for other religions.

Now-a-days, the word "Secular Stare" is being used as opposed to a theocratic state. The adoption of this word is a mere imitation of the western thought-pattern. We had no need to import it. We called it a secular state to contrast it with Pakistan. There is some misunderstanding arising out of this. Religion was equated with Dharma, and the secular state was meant to be a state without Dharma. Some said, ours is a state without Dharma, whereas others trying to find a better sounding word called it *Dharma-nirapeksha* (indifferent to Dharma) State. But all these words are fundamentally erroneous. For, a state can neither be without Dharma nor can it be indifferent to Dharma, just as fire cannot be without heat. If fire loses heat, it does not remain fire any longer. State, which exists fundamentally to maintain Dharma, to maintain law and order, can neither be without Dharma nor indifferent to Dharma. If it is, it will be a lawless state, and where there is lawlessness, where is the question of the existence of any state? In other words, concepts of *Dharma-nirapekshata* (attitude of indifference towards Dharma) and state are self-contradictory. State can only be a *Dharma-Rajya* (rule of Dharma), and nothing else. Any other definition will go against the very *raison d'etre* of the state.

In a *Dharma-Rajya* the state is not absolutely powerful. It is subject to *Dharma. S*overeignty is vested in Dharma. Presently there has arisen a controversy. Whether the parliament is sovereign or the Supreme Court, and whether the Legislature is higher or the Judiciary. This is like a quarrel as to whether the left hand is more important or the right hand? Both are the limbs of the state, the Legislature as well as Judiciary. Both have distinct functions to perform. In their individual sphere each is supreme. To consider either one above the other would be a mistake. Yet the legislators say, "We are higher". On the other hand, members of the Judiciary assert that they have a higher authority, since they interpret the laws which the Legislature makes. The Legislature claims to have given powers to the Judiciary. If necessary, Legislature can change the Constitution. In reality, both the Legislature and the Judiciary are on an equal plane. Neither the Legislature is higher nor the Judiciary. *Dharma* is higher than both. The Legislature will have to act according to *Dharma* and the Judiciary too will have to act according to *Dharma. Dharma* will specify limits of both. The Legislature, the Judiciary, or the people, none of these is supreme. Some will say "Why ! People are sovereign. They elect". But even the people are not sovereign because people too have no right to act against *Dharma.* If an elected government allows people to go against *dharma* and does not punish, then that government is in reality a government of thieves. Even the General will cannot go against *Dharma.* Imagine what will be the situation if, by some manoeuvring, thieves gain a majority in the government and send one from their ranks as the head of executive. What will be the duty of the minority if the majority is of thieves and elects a thief to rule ? The duty clearly will be to remove the representative elected by the majority.

During the Second World War when Hitler attacked France, the French army could not stall the onward march of Nazi troops. The then Prime Minister of France, Marshall Petain, decided to surrender. The French public supported the decision, but de Gaulle escaped to London where he declared that he did not accept the surrender; France is independent and will remain so. From London, he formed a Government of France in exile and eventually liberated

France. Now if the majority rule is to be considered supreme, then de Gaulle's action will have to be condemned. He had no right to fight in the name of independence. de Gaulle derived his right from the fact that the French nation was above the majority public opinion. The national *Dharma is* above all. Independence is *Dharma* of every nation. It is the duty of every citizen to preserve independence, and to strive for regaining it when it is lost. Even in our country, the majority had not risen against the Britishers; only a few had. Some revolutionaries sprang up, some brave people stood and fought. The Lokmanya declared, "Freedom is my Birthright". He did not declare this birthright with the support of a majority or a referendum of the people. Elections and majority can decide as to who will form the government. The truth cannot be decided by the majority. What the government will do will be decided by *Dharma.*[13]

All know that in the USA, where Americans swear by democracy, Lincoln did not accept wrong public opinion on the question of the abolition of slavery. When the Southern states declared their intention to secede, Lincoln stood firm and told them: "You have no right to secede even in a democracy". He fought against this and did not allow them to secede. Nor did he, tolerate slavery. He did not show readiness for a compromise whereby there might continue partial slavery to accommodate Southern states. He did not favour the policy of compromise. He categorically declared that the system of slavery was against tradition, the Dharma, the principles which were at the basis of American nation. Therefore, the system of slavery had to be abolished. When the Southerners decided to secede, he told them: "You cannot secede". On this point there was a civil war and Lincoln did not compromise with *adharma.*

Let us understand *very* clearly that Dharma is not necessarily with the majority or with the people. *Dharma* is eternal. Therefore, it is not enough to say, while defining democracy, that it is, the government of the people. It has to be a government for the good of the people. What constitutes the good of the people ? It is *Dharma* alone, which can decide. Therefore, a democratic government, *Jana Rajya,* must also be rooted in *Dharma,* i.e. must be a *Dharma Rajya.* In the definition of Democracy, *viz.* "government of the people, by the people, and for the people", 'of' stands for independence, 'by' stands for democracy, and 'for' indicates Dharma. Therefore, there is true democracy only where there is freedom as well as *Dharma. Dharma-Rajya* encompasses all these concepts.[14]

REFERENCES

1. Hobbes, Thomas, *Leviathan* (London: Arnold), 1947; Locke, John, *Of Civil Governments* (London: Dent); 1943, Rousseau, Jean Jacques, *Social Contract* (Harmondsworth: Penguin Books), 1984.
2. McDougal, William, *Group Mind* (Cambridge: Cambridge University Press), 1920, p. 26.
3. Golwalkar, M.S., *Deendayal Upadhyaya and D.B. Thengadi, Integral Approach* (New Delhi: Suruchi Prakashan), 1991, p. 34.
4. *Ibid.*, p 35.
5. Bhishikar, C.P., *Pandit Deendayal Upadhyaya, Ideology and Perception*, Part V, *Concept of Rashtriya* (New Delhi: Suruchi Prakashan), 1991.
6. Golwalkar, M.S., *Deendayal Upadhyaya and D.B. Thengadi, Integral Approach, op. cit.*, pp. 38-39.
7. Nene, V.V., *Pandit Deendayal Upadhyaya, Ideology and Perception*, Part II, *Integral Humanism, op. cit.*, p. 58.
8. Golwalkar, M.S., *Deendayal Upadhyaya and D.B. Thengadi, Integral Approach, op. cit.*, p. 43.
9. Deodhar, V.N., *Pandit Deendayal Upadhyaya, Ideology and Perception*, Part VII, *A Profile* (New Delhi: Suruchi Publications), 1991, p. 53.
10. Golwalkar, M.S., *Deendayal Upadhyaya and D.B. Thengadi, Integral Approach, op. cit.*, p. 44.
11. Jog, B.N., *Pandit Deendayal Upadhyaya, Ideology and Perception*, Part VI, *Politics for Nation's Sake* (New Delhi: Suruchi Publications), 1991, pp. 20 - 30.
12. *Ibid.*, pp. 74-80.
13. Golwalkar, M.S., *Deendayal Upadhyaya and D.B. Thengadi, Integral Approach, op. cit.*, pp. 53-54.
14. *Ibid.*

5

CONCEPT OF RASHTRA

When we speak of Deendayal's thoughts, his analysis, his inferences, the term 'his' does not have a restrictive specific or distinctive connotation. In the case of men like Deendayal, it is difficult to separate their thoughts from their life and actions. Our national tradition speaks through them. Thinkers and philosophers like Deendayal through their extraordinary genius, give only a new expression, in the light of the modern context, to those ideals and abiding philosophy which flowered in this soil for thousands of years and whose continuity thrived against all odds. They are modern exponents of our eternal national philosophy. The basic principles they propagate are not new. They are motivated by the sincere urge to remove the self-oblivion of their people and to awaken its consciousness and urge to act.

If we look at Panditji's life from this point of view, we will not fail to mark that in addition to his in-born piercing, probing intelligence, he was considerably benefited by years of national *sanskaras.* He came in contact with the *Rashtriya Swayamsevak Sangh* in 1937, and was completely absorbed in that work till 1951. During this period, his analytical power, thinking capacity and mode of living developed with a firm foundation. He came into close contact with M.S. Golwalkar Sarsanghachalak of the RSS. and completely identified him self with the RSS ideology. He was completely lost in his devotion to the Motherland. The *Hindu Rashtra* ideology, unequivocally accepted by the RSS, is basic to Deendayal's thinking. The expression *'Hindu Rashtra'* and the basic principles of the *Hindu Rashtra* as an ideology were not invented by the

RSS. Dr. K.B. Hedgewar, the founder of RSS, accepted the ideology of cultural nationalism, so clearly perceived and expressed by Swami Vivekanand, Shri Aurobindo, Lokamanya Tilak, Swatantryaveer Savarkar and others.[1] Territorial nationalism implies that the Indian nation is formed of all those people who reside on this land. Nowhere in the world is this concept of 'Nation' a coincident with a particular territory and accepted by all the people residing there. In our country, however, the term 'Indian', popularised by the Westerners to facilitate pronunciation, created great confusion. The historical and natural identity between 'Hindu' and 'Hindustan' was cast aside; the term 'Hindi' was sought to be equated with the term 'Indian'. 'Indian Nationalism' came to mean 'Hindi Rashtravad' (Hindi nationalism). An effort was consistently made to look upon Hindus, Muslims, Christians etc. as 'nationals' and forge them into an integrated force against the alien rule. Yet the confusion regarding nationhood was hardly felt till 1920, when the Congress under the leadership of Gandhiji adopted the Khilafat movement: Appeasement of the Muslims had not yet become part of the Congress policy.[2] It was in the following years, however, that Muslim communalism became more and more aggressive and dogmatic on the one hand, and on the other, Congress leaders carried the idea of Hindu-Muslim unity to a ridiculous extent in the name of national interest. This is not the place to go into the details of the historical process. Suffice it to say that the pure and simple concept of nationalism came to be more and more distorted during the freedom movement between 1920 and 1947, and that prominent leaders tried to claim that the distorted idea was the real national concept. Any other way of thinking was branded as communal. The true devotees of the Motherland came to be regarded as communal and parochial in their own land.

When Hedgewar proclaimed that India is a *Hindu Rashtra,* it was because he clearly visualised the imminent danger to the future of the nation that this ideological confusion was likely to create. Hindus form nation in Hindustan and their organisation must consequently be regarded as a national organisation. He came to the firm conclusion that unless the Hindu society became united and strong, our nation will not be able to finally overcome the threat to its very existence. He founded the RSS with national reconstruction as its goal. Panditji not only accepted this line of thinking, he also made it the subject of his constant meditation, study and deep dedication. He tried to reach the roots of the problem, the historic concept of the nature of this nation developed through centuries, its fundamental values, its reconstruction for the future. The nationalistic thought of the RSS was completely assimilated by him, and when, in reverence to Golwalkar wishes, he accepted the work of the political party, he naturally went on propounding, even in the political field, the theory identifying the Hindu way of life with the national way of life, instead of getting misguided by the popular theory of territorial nationalism. He was thoroughly convinced of the correctness of this ideology of cultural nationhood.

Lack of Swadeshi (Indigenous) Thinking

In this way, Deendayal imbibed the line of RSS reasoning about the way in which harmful tendencies were increasingly nourished after the achievement of independence of partitioned India in 1947. He clearly saw that in our Constitution, economic policies, goals of development, of the social structure, our models of building a glorious nation, there was no trace of indigenous thinking, Bharat is an ancient land with thousands of years of history behind it. Great, selfless seers here have given deep thought to the purpose of human life, from the social as well as individual point of view. There doesn't seem to be any awareness now that we can search for and decide our future course in the light of this precious heritage. At one place, Panditji has given a very effective expression to this agony when he writes: "We became free in 1947. The English quit India. We felt that what was considered to be the greatest obstacle in the path of our effort of nation-building was removed, and were all of a sudden faced with the problem as to what the significance of this hard earned independence was. What pattern of life do we want to develop here ? As a nation, what are our ideals and our criteria for a meaningful existence ? Since we had no clear vision of our true national identity here, we could not utilize political freedom to realise our national ideals. We aped the foreigners to such an extent that we failed to see that our inherent national ideals and traditions should be reflected in our Constitution. We satisfied ourselves with making a patch work of theories and principles enunciated in the foreign countries. We have not yet been able to answer the basic question as to what kind of life we want to develop here. Because we failed to grasp the real Spirit of our national life, we could not stand on our own legs. True, we made great efforts to attain national prosperity, but we failed miserably to understand what our ideal of national glory consists of, and how it should manifest itself in our onward march. Many have attempted to answer this question and yet we come to the same conclusion, that their thoughts have so far been based mostly on foreign ways of living and thinking. Some of them desire to build our society on the socialistic pattern, some on the communistic pattern; some speak of democratic socialism in which there is an effort for synthesis of socialism and individual freedom. All these efforts seem to have their genesis in patterns imported from foreign countries. In all walks of life, economic, political, social, all our thinking is based on foreign concepts. Our planners believe, as it were, that at no time has deep thought been given to these things in our ancient national traditions or that our national life is a product only of the past few years. The result was that our national culture and traditions were never at all reflected in these ideologies borrowed from elsewhere, and so they utterly failed to touch the chords of our national being. These foreign thoughts would never inspire our people for self-sacrifice, hard work and total dedication. This has led to a mood of frustration in the people. The nation's confidence has been shaken. We have lost our incentive for hard work and thus our great society of crores of people has become a living example of complete dependence on others."[3]

The Basis of Cultural Unity

Deendayal never compromised on his clear and unequivocal use of phrases like "our ancient nation", "our idea of a glorious life", "the philosophy of life here developed through the ages", "national self-respect" and "national character".[4] Above all, he made a clear exposition of our nationhood in a lucid and logically convincing manner. It is essential that we should properly understand the direction of his thinking in this respect. For it is only a clear understanding of the philosophy underlying our national life that can bring about a proper national reawakening. The education imposed in the days of the British, false and misleading theories which were deliberately disseminated, the tendency among our educated people blindly to accept these theories, the wrong policies adopted by the Congress party in the pre-independence period and the dogged propagation of the utterly misleading concept of nationalism by the then leaders for their selfish political ends even after the attainment of independence—all these led to the complete distorted connotation of the terms communalism and nationalism. The primary need for the rebuilding of our nation is to free the national mind from this confusion and to provide a natural, positive content to their concept of nationhood. Two things are achieved if a clear concept of nationhood is developed. Firstly, everyone has a proper criterion to judge national interest; secondly, efforts for progress in all walks of life get the right direction because of the constant awareness of our national ethos. Once we are clear about what values are vital, we can work for a prosperous future while adhering to our characteristic national qualities and our nation's mission, and maintaining continuity in our past, present and future.

To sum up, Deendayal, giving full consideration to thousands of years of our nation's history, looks upon cultural unity as the basis of our existence as a nation. What culture does he imply ? Call it *Arya Sanskriti!,* or Bharatiya or Vedic culture or whatever other name you like for it is in the final analysis, Hindu culture. This culture was developed by people who were known in this land as the Hindus and so it has existed without doubt, as *Hindu Rashtra* from times immemorial. This is not a new discovery made by Panditji; from the earliest times we see that cultural unity is the foundation of our existence as one nation. Different political systems prevailed in this country at different times. Powerful kings built extensive empires under one rule in this land. A number of small States also existed in different parts of the country. The country had to face foreign aggressions and saw moments of triumph as well as defeat. Yet, there rarely was any confusion (at least till the onset of the

British regime) about who were our nationals here and who were the aliens. Even when the Hindus loyally served the aggressors, they were completely conscious that it was the foreigner that they served. The idea that we are building a new nation or that a new nation is emerging here is totally wrong. The nationhood that Bharat attained was not due to the mere existence of a people in this land. The notion that a nation is formed of all those people who live within certain territorial boundaries is not accepted anywhere in the world; the Congress tried to popularise it here. But it can certainly not be applied to an ancient nation like Bharatvarsha.[5]

Difference in Developmental Process

Most of the Western countries were born in the recent past, i.e. during the last four hundred years or so. The tests we may apply to their nationhood are not completely relevant to Bharat ; nor can we compare the process of their development with that of Bharat.

While talking about India with reference to the Western countries, it would be desirable to take into consideration some basic facts. First, things like the emergence of love for the nation, unity, integration and their growth were not the result of a reaction to any particular circumstances or events; it is entirely inherent, positive and born out of the selfless thinking of our ancient sages and seers. Even a casual glance at Western nationalism shows that its birth and development have arisen as a reaction to certain circumstances. The first thing that strikes us in this regard is that people occupying the European territory were mainly followers of the Christian faith. Nothing like the feeling of nationalism had developed among them. The Pope's rule was supreme everywhere. In the Western terminology, we can say that religion and religious institutions completely dominated the whole of Europe. Gradually, however, people came to resent Pope's interference in their everyday worldly affairs as well as their modes of worship, and they started looking upon Pope as a foreign imperialistic power. This reaction against Papal power gave birth to the ideas of nation and nationalism. Thus, as we have said earlier, nationalism in Europe was a reactionary feeling. This feeling of nationalism and the power of Pope could simply not co-exist peacefully. This reactionary patriotism was also detrimental to international tolerance and peaceful co-existence. It was competitive, selfish and egotistic; it was conducive to the exploitation of the weak. As a result, a clear antagonism developed between nationalism and inter-nationalism.[6] In addition to this, every nation accepted free competition among its constituents, leading to two conflicting classes—the exploiters and the exploited. This tendency became more and more unbridled with the growth of the machine-dominated civilization. Even small children became victims of the industrial revolution. It was inevitable that this extreme, intolerant, and uncultured nationalism and craving for profit, in its turn, led to another reaction. The result of this reaction was the birth of the communist ideology which spurned the very concepts of religion, nationalism and nationhood. An international movement based on class struggle was launched. The question is: how far would it be logical and just to presume that the same process must have taken place in Bharat also ? The concept of nationalism is a positive development in India, which took place at a time when the new concept of nationalism was not even born in other parts of the world. The Bharatiya concept is essentially different in nature and is aimed at taking humanity towards a definite goal of achievement.

All known history has, from the hoary past, looked upon Bharat as a well-knit nation. All known and unknown history has for all time recognised the relation between this land and its people as that of mother and sons. In the course of time, a number of upheavals took place, but the same cultural main stream had an uninterrupted sway here. This cultural stream embraces literature like the Vedas, the Upanishads, the Ramayana and the Mahabharat, the seers and sages who by their penance bestowed upon *Bharat-Bhoomi* the purity of a sacred land of self-realisation, an unbroken chain of valiant heroes and a set of National Values manifested through all these facets. Bharatiya culture has been enriched through the synthesis of all these. This culture has developed an inner unity and a sense of belonging in this society. In the long stream of its history the Hindus have shared the experience of identical happiness and misery and moments of triumph and humiliation; they had an extensive tradition of spiritual leaders and brave warriors; nursed similar aspirations about their motherland and have existed here as a nation in the real sense of the term. In order to form a nation, it is necessary to have a people living in a common territory to make up a nation. So also are a certain emotional integration, an identity of national sentiments and an internal sharing of life-purpose essential. All the people living in a certain territory are not necessarily its nationals.[7]

Truth Established by History

He says, "A nation is not a mere geographical unit. The primary need of nationalism is the feeling of boundless dedication in the hearts of the people for their land. It is because of this feeling of affection that we call it our Motherland. Our feeling for the Motherland has a basis: our long, continuous habitation in the same land creates, by association, a deep sense of 'my-ness'. Gradually, a common national history is developed. Some events involve our triumph, some our humiliation. The memories of our glorious deeds make us proud; ignominies make us hang our heads in shame. The memories of the aggressions by Mohammed Ghori or Mahammed Ghaznavi naturally fill us with agony. We develop a feeling of attachment for Prithviraj and other patriots. If, instead, any person feels pride for the aggressors and no love for the Motherland, he can lay no claim to patriotism. The memory of Rana Pratap, Chhatrapati Shivaji, or Guru Govind Singh makes us bow down our heads with respect and devotion. On the other hand, with the very mention of the names of Aurangzeb and Allauddin, Clive or Dalhousie, we are filled with feelings of anger that are natural towards foreign aggressors. Thus, a nation is formed of people who live in a certain land, whose hearts are filled with pure love and dedication for the Motherland, whose ideals of life are similar, who have a certain common philosophy of life, whose ideas about their friends and foes are the same, and who share a common set of heroes and leaders in history."[8]

There is really no ground for the least doubt in anybody's mind about the fact that Indian nationalism is Hindu nationalism. Which society looks upon this land as its Motherland? or worships her fervently like a goddess ? or remember her again and again saying

त्वं दुर्गा दशप्रहरणधारिणी ('You are Durga, wielding ten weapons')? or has the same national heroes in history? Which society, if it is asked to choose between Rana Pratap and Akbar as their national hero, instinctively answers 'Rana Pratap'? Which society has a common view of life? However, many questions are asked, the one inevitable answer is unequivocally—'The Hindu Society'. This is a most positive stand. When the European society was divided into various nationalities, the Western thinker tried to define the term 'nation'. Efforts were made to make a list of those constituents which are responsible for arousing the basic feeling of nationalism in the minds of crores of people.[9] Many learned volumes were written on this subject. Western thinkers tell us: Nationalism as a political force is a product of the French Revolution and the situation created by it. Western writers have mentioned various constituents which go to make a nation, such as common race, language, religion, land, traditions, common calamities, means of transport, common political administration, etc. It is their observation that the common existence of one or more predominant features among these goes to make and preserve a nation. No one has been able to name a definite set of all those constituents which apply to all the nations in the world. We see that race, language and religion are not common constituents which are universally applicable to all nations. Europe, following the same religion, is made up of various nations. In spite of the multiplicity of religions, Bharat is one nation. There are examples like Czechoslovakia where a number of ethnic groups have come together and formed a nation. This analysis has primarily been limited only to nations in Western Europe, but the study of nations like Bharat has found no place in it. Nation in Europe do not appear to have been formed at any one time or because of any particular set of reasons. The process started with England in the XVI century, and we see a nation like Bulgaria appearing for the first time on the map of the world as late as 1908. We must always bear in mind that there is a basic difference between the Western concept of nation—which has arisen out of a machine-dominated civilisation full of brute strength and conflict—and a totally different Hindu concept of nation. Considering that the inherent consciousness of unity, identical ties of history and tradition, relations of affinity between the land and the people, and the same aspirations and hopes as broadly acceptable constituents, we reach the selfcame conclusion that Hindustan is a nation of the Hindus. None in the world would accept that a hotch-potch of people living in the same land but following mutually opposed ways of life and aspirations. can be regarded as a Nation. There is no gainsaying the fact, whichever way we look at it, that *Hindutva* alone is the basis of nationalism in Bharat, remains unhampered. It is altogether wrong for the Hindus to prove their nationhood by European standards. It has been accepted as axiomatic for thousands of years.

The foundation for Deendayal's theory of nationhood was the Motherland, people's devotion to the Motherland and the cultural stream providing the unifying factor. According to him, national integration really meant, first, strengthening the feeling of affinity among those who are naturally part of the stream of Hindu Culture and secondly, to bring those who stray away from it in the Hindu cultural stream and assimilate them in that mainstream. The currents which have been cut off from the mainstream will automatically grow weak and dry up. This mainstream naturally possesses the characteristic feature of assimilating all. So, to look upon Sikhs, Jains, Boudhs, Harijans and *Vanavasis* as separate social groups as apart from the Hindu mainstream is to weaken the unifying principle and to promote disintegration. On the wide stage of national life, all these have an equal status. They are all organs of the Hindu society. Though various organs of the body serve different functions, they together form a healthy body. There is no dearth today of forces which encourage the disintegrating elements with a desire that the Indian nation should not remain healthy and should grow weaker and progressively more diseased. These forces of disintegration are both internal and foreign.

This is one approach to equality. The other approach also is closely tied up with this thought and with Hindu philosophy.[10]

विष्णुमय जग वैष्णवाचा धर्म।
भेदभाव भ्रम अमंगल।।

(The world is all permeated by Lord Vishnu : so equality is the *dharma* of the Vaishnavas. All discrimination is an illusion and therefore, unholy). Or

भक्ति एथ सरे जाति अप्रमाण

(Devotion here spreads everywhere alike. Castes do not provide a criterion).

In these and other *abhangas* (devotional songs) the influence of the same philosophical thought of spiritual unity is reflected, and it has for its basis the knowledge and experience that the spirit in all beings is one.

जे जे देखिजे भूत ते मानिजे भगवन्त

(Every being you see should be looked upon as God).

This is the attitude springing from this experience but the actuality in the everyday life of the ordinary common man is that instead of this unity, social inequality and feeling of high and low prevail. While working for a national organisation, the problem today is how to eradicate this inequality and feeling of alienation and to establish equality in day-to-day social life. Workers engaged in the task of organisation are irked by this mental and psychological obstacle in their persistent effort for Hindu unity. The position today is that a large neglected section of the Hindu society is inclined to disown Hinduism and retaliate by any means against those who consider themselves high-caste. The atmosphere has become explosive. Legislation has proved ineffective in this regard. Even for the solution of this problem one has to revert to the answer provided by Panditji. The right approach is to look upon the nation as the focal point, give the maximum scope for individual development and follow the path of harmony and cooperation rather than that of conflict. To welcome and accommodate one and all in the wide expanse of Hinduism in a dignified manner, to imbibe a sense of unity in every heart, to discard old, outdated distorted systems and replace them by modern ones suitable to the times, would be in keeping with the Hindu view of life. RSS has provided a model of such a corporate living. To expand it hundred-fold and to strengthen the bonds of affinity for the purpose is the practical aspect of this answer.

Discretion in Equality

Even though slogans of equality are raised in the modern world, the concept of equality has to be accepted with discretion. Our actual experience is that from the practical and material point of view, no two men are alike. Their looks and colour of skin and their physical built are different as are their inherent qualities. Considerable bitterness could be avoided, if the idea of equality as conceived by Hindu thinkers is studied more carefully. The first and basic premise is that even if men have different qualities and different kinds of duties allotted to them according to their qualities or aptitudes, all duties are equally dignified. This is called *Swadharma,* and there is an unequivocal assurance that to follow *swadharma is* itself equivalent to the worship of God. So, in any duties performed to fulfil *swadharma,* the question of high and low, dignified and undignified does not arise at all. If the duty is done without selfishness, no blame attaches itself to the doer. This really is the real concept of dignity of labour. We see that our well known saints in the path of *bhakti* belong to various occupational groups. And in the end, all of them achieved the identical highest fruition in life. The other practical consideration is that the structure of man's life has to be inevitably organised according to some principle for the stability, character and unimpeded development of society. Some people endowed with certain qualities, rise to responsible positions and become leaders in various fields. If a man belongs to this category, he naturally enjoys more dignity than what the other ordinary common people do. The higher prestigious positions today are posts like the President of the Indian Republic, Prime Minister, Minister, a Chairman of an institution or organisation. But there is bitter competition for such posts. Many social groups desire that one of their members should occupy the highest post. Why ? Because power, money, luxuries and status are all concentrated in that post. Not only power, but many perquisites like a bungalow, car, domestic servants, travel at government expense, free telephone, furniture and other facilities accompany a minister's post as a corollary. There are opportunities for him to fill his coffers. On the other hand, our ancient system or structure was based on a different principle : the higher the post, the fewer the opportunities for wealth and luxuries. Rishis and saints commanded so great a prestige that at their arrival, the king would rise and offer them an exalted seat first and humbly bow to them. They would spell out the rules of social life based on dharma. But their own daily life had to be free from pleasure, attachments and luxuries and entirely dedicated to God. They took care to see that their character was absolutely unblemished and devoid of all desire for sensual enjoyment.

We have any number of examples of highly respected, ascetic-minded great men on whose shoulders fell the mantle of high position in connection with their society or nation. They had inherent aptitude not to get involved in material wealth, and even to discard it. Arya Chanakya adorned the position of Chandragupta's chief minister for some time; he manoeuvred the fall of the unrighteous Nanda rule, but he never gave up his simple life in the hut. The moment he got a capable minister like Rakshasa to work for Chandragupta, he voluntarily relinquished his ministership and dedicated himself to god-realisation. Kunti was the Queen Dowager. When the Pandavas won the War and Yudhishthira ascended the throne, Kunti decided to adopt Vanaprastha ashram and left for the forest. Yudhishthira asked her, "You continually goaded us on to the war. Why then, immediately after our attainment of the throne, are you leaving us?" At this Kunti replied, "You are Kshatriyas, and as such it was my duty to urge you to fulfil your responsibility. It was your duty to fight against *adharma* and you did it. I have no desire whatsoever for royal pomp and glory. To become a *vanaprastha ashrami* and accompany my brother-in-law to the .forest is now my *swadharma*. Bharata in the Ramayana was detachment incarnate. He kept Rama's *padukas* (footwear) on the throne and officiated as a king for fourteen years. He could easily have usurped the throne. Rama would never have asked him to return his kingdom to him. And Bharata agreed to officiate as king only on condition that if Rama did not return after the stipulated time, he would have a pyre lit to immolate himself, in fact he was on the point of doing so when Rama returned. Rama and Krishna did not do anything for personal aggrandisement. They observed *karmayoga*. They behaved thus, keeping in view the principle

यद् यद् आचरति श्रेष्ठस्तद् तदेवेतरो जनः ।

(Ordinary people follow the path followed by great men.)

Such behaviour leaves no scope for inequality or jealousy. When a post becomes the means to satisfy the hunger for luxury and social status, the result is exploitation, conflict and corruption increase, and the atmosphere is vitiated. So in our culture, that leadership is looked upon as genuine which is unrelated to political or economic power and is based on moral authority. Such leadership can in times of need exercise a deterrent control on the rulers and on government machinery. This is what we call ऋषि-शक्ति (moral or saintly force). In the present situation, perhaps, such a force will have to be raised in the form of non-political organisations, since people who assume power seem now to forget the basic *Rajadharma* which consists of caring for the material prosperity of the subjects and giving them the security needed for spiritual upliftment. Their tendency is towards unrestrained use of power for selfish ends. At such times an independent moral or saintly force restraining the rulers becomes imperative.

In the orginal system, ordinary workers, peasants, traders and professionals had greater scope for material comforts and luxuries, but they did not enjoy the prestige that the ascetic rulers or *sannyasis* had. The stream of knowledge and character percolated from higher levels to downwards, while material-facilities progressively decreased from the lowest to the top. The result was that everyone was satisfied in his own way. No one felt jealous of another, and whatever he lacked in one field was made up for in another. No one insisted that he must get the prestige of the rishis without performing penance like them. Everyone had the opportunity of choosing his own path according to his own ability and develop to the highest positions of the fruition of life. The path of salvation was wide open for every single individual. Since we do not see this in actual reality anywhere today, we find even its comprehension somewhat difficult.

Hindutva: A Matter of Pride

It must be said that this Indian idea of equality is more natural, more prone to progress, closer to human sentiment, more satisfying, and useful in raising the qualitative stature of the whole society, than the Western idea of equality tending to enforce uniformity. It is of course taken for granted that in any system, everyone must have the certainty of securing the primary and common necessities of life, like food, clothing, shelter, education, medical aid etc. If the common people are confident about getting these, further progress can be uninterrupted, except for individual exceptions. It is a mistaken notion of equality if we go on multiplying our needs and then, expect equality in their fulfilment. The main principle behind social justice is that no one should be exploited, and the gains of prosperity should be shared by all. If, with this all-comprehensive thought in mind, everyone practises equality and breaks away from all pride (according to the tenets suggested by the saints), there will be no room for unhealthy competition, jealousy, bitterness, hatred, conflict, neglect etc. which can lead to the disintegration of society. If harmonious coordination and complementariness, the basic foundations of the Hindu way of life, are kept in mind and the social fabric is woven accordingly, the seeds of poison which the enemies of the Hindu society nourish for their benefit will be destroyed and a healthy society. brimming with energy and enthusiasm will take shape. It was the distinctive feature of the *Hindu Rashtra* that it built a harmonious design in the life of the people by striking a balance between apparent contraries like sacrifice and indulgence, distribution and consumption, equality and discrimination, and give individual and social life a proper direction.

But this pure and healthy character of social structure was lost sight of and this led to the creation of several distortions and unbearable evils in it. If we study carefully the basic philosophy and the actual life of the people in the Western and communist countries, we fail to discover anything in them to attract us. It is not in the nature of *Hindu Rashtra* to guage the status and prestige of human life by the vulgar show of material opulence, licentiousness in the name of individual freedom and the existence of man as an economic animal controlled by the comprehensive domination of a totalitarian regime. The traditions of *Hindu Rashtra* are entirely different.

Our way consists of the concept of the totality of Man, the stable, balanced development of individual and social life on that basis and everyone's happiness, motivation of spiritual satisfaction and attainment of collective prosperity for the nation consequent to it. Our freedom should really have led to the deepening of our faith in our way of life and the concentration of our attention on reorganising our life pattern. If this longing for self-realisation were awakened, the infinite dormant strength of our *Hindu Rashtra* would burst forth in its life.

If the word Hindu, with this noble content is properly understood, there is no reason why we should be ashamed of being Hindus; on the contrary we should take pride in it. Deendayal has freely used the words *Hindu Rashtra,* Bharat, Bharatiya, Hindustan as synonyms. Not that he was oblivious of the fact that some people purposely attach the charge of communalism, narrow parochialism, obscurantism to these words. But he was never in two minds about asserting that the word Bharatiya means Hindu. Indeed, in some cases while referring to *Bharatiya Sanskriti*, he purposely writes in brackets, i.e. 'Hindu Sanskriti' so that the readers should have no confusion. As a matter of fact there need not be any confusion, yet we find it prevailing. The reason is that the Congress leaders and so-called progressive thinkers influenced by Western thought did not and still do not translate Indian culture as 'Hindu Sanskriti'. Pandit Nehru believed that India is a nation, but he claimed that there exists a composite culture here. He saw different cultures in different places. He did not accept the obvious truth that the entire Bharat stands together on the sole basis of its Hindu culture. He thought it the very limit of folly to call this nation a *Hindu Rashtra.* The same argument is adopted by the so-called 'progressives' of the Congress, Socialist and Communist groups. The fact that Rashtriya Swayamsevak Sangh organises the Hindus and yet calls itself 'national' or *Rashtriya* is to them altogether paradoxical. They think the words *Hindubhoomi* and *Hindu rashtraangabhoota* (constituents of *Hindu Rashtra)* appearing in the Sangh prayers are narrow or parochial. There are a number of sympathisers of RSS also who advise the RSS to adopt the words *Bharat* and *Bharatiya* in place of Hindustan and Hindu. But RSS looks on these words Bharatiya and Hindu as synonyms. The impact of the age old British policy is obvious in the phrase "India that is Bharat." There is behind it a crafty conscious effort to make the Hindus forget their past. As a matter of fact, when we use the words Bharat, Bharatiya Rashtra, Bharatiya Sanskriti, what else do they signify except the Hindu? When foreign scholars come here to study Indian culture, what do they study ? They have no reason to come to India to study Muslim or Christian culture. For that they can better go to Turkey, Mecca or Medina or the Vatican City in Rome. They really desire to come to India and conduct research in Hindu traditions, ancient Sanskrit literature and the life-values accepted by the ancient traditions here.[11]

The Foundation: A National Organisation

Those who advise giving up the word Hindu, either feel that the word narrows down our nation-concept or find that the word is inexpedient for them in their competitive politics. They are afraid that they would loose the votes of millions of Christians and Muslim voters. Their misconception is that the use of the word *Hindu Rashtra* excludes Muslim and Christian communities. If both these communities become one with the national cultural stream without any change in their mode of worship, if they own the ancient tradition here, if they look upon our national heroes as their national heroes and if they develop devotion for Bharat Mata as their Motherland with undivided fidelity, they will of course be nationals here. But somehow this thought does not occur to them. As a matter of fact, this insistence is most essential from the point of national integration. Newspapermen and political leaders use the term Indian Muslims or Indian Christians as a matter of habit, but while doing so their residence in Bharat and their citizenship are taken for granted. But should an Indian Muslim not be a Hindu Muslim and an Indian Christian a Hindu Christian ? Golwalkar used to put forth this line of thinking in the clearest possible terms.[12] It will mean that Hindu is the nationality and Muslim is a sect. It will mean that they accept the value system in India and own the responsibility of putting that system into practice. The word Indian today connotes only the territorial citizenship of India. It does not connote the qualitative content or manifest the distinctive national characteristics.[13]

Such mistaken notions and policies have led the whole country into a mess which cannot be cleared up without an uncompromising and fearless advocacy of Hindu Nationalism. Panditji tried to explain to the people with the courage of his conviction the maxim that the basis of an organisation is the Nation, and in the Indian context 'Nation' means the Hindu nation or *Hindu Rashtra.* There was not even the least of reactionary element in his assertion. He never once said that Hindus should organise themselves or insist on Hindutva because the Muslims or Christians behave in this or that way. On the other hand, he argued that many ills gripped the Hindu society; the people forgot their duty to the nation, became selfish. and indulged in internal conflict leading to our exploitation by the foreigners. He had looked upon *Hindu Rashtra,* and the organisation of Hindus for its prosperity, as a natural and positive need of the hour. It is certainly not because he has enemies to fight with, that a man tries to become healthy and develop strength. A healthy body is a *dharmasadhana,* an instrument for living according to *dharma.* Our approach has been expressed in the statement शरीर माद्यं खलु धर्मसाधनम् (The body is the primary instrument of dharma.) The call for an organised Hindu society has nothing in common with Western type organisations: peasants and workers should organise themselves to fight against exploitation; Russia and America should pile up stores of nuclear arms in fear of each other; women should organise themselves to fight male oppression. Deendayal never once suggested this approach. While pondering over the essentials of our national life, he became conscious of some distortions that had developed in it and drew pointed attention to them and depicted a clear picture of healthy national life. All his life, he placed before the nation the thought that whatever may be the causes of our social ills—it may be blind imitation of the foreigners, or self-oblivion, or ignorance, or a thousand years of slavery—they must be eradicated and our nation must be nourished with the life-giving sap of Hindu idealism. It must become healthy and glorious so as to fulfil its world mission. Bharat Mata was not to him a subject for compromise or bargain or political expediency. It was to him an article of faith, a subject of extreme devotion and dedication. It was in this sense that he was different from the current political stream and he was pledged to make Herculean efforts so as to give proper direction to the flow of events. He was bent on dispelling all darkness, by spreading the light of self-evident nationalism of a constructive, untarnished kind, unaffected by changes in external circumstances. The word *Bharatiya* has been wrongly used to propagate a new definition of nationhood in the last fifty or sixty years. The word has lost the inspiring and enlightening value-oriented content. The word Hindu suggests a human ideology embracing the entire universe. Unfortunately, the word 'Bharatiya' is used in such a way that this content is narrowed down. Deendayal's insistence is that unless we stick fast and with conviction to the word Hindu, the twin objectives of national integration and the emergence of an organised society will never be attained.[14]

REFERENCES

1. Andersen, Walter K., and Shridhar, D. Damle, *The Brotherhood in Saffron, The Rashtriya Swayamsevak Sangh and Hindu Revivalism* (New Delhi: Vistaar Publications), 1987, pp. 27-28.
2. Bhishikar, C.P., *Pandit Deendayal Upadhyaya, Ideology and Perception*, Part V, *Concept of Rashtriya, op. cit.*, p. 19.
3. *Rashtrya Dharma*, November-December, 1951.
4. Bhishikar, C.P., *Pandit Deendayal Upadhyaya, Ideology and Perception*, Part V, *Concept of Rashtriya, op. cit.*, p. 22.
5. *Organiser*, July 6, 1961.
6. Golwalkar, M.S., *Deendayal Upadhyaya and D.B. Thengadi, Integral Approach, op. cit.*, p. 18.
7. Bhishikar, C.P., *Pandit Deendayal Upadhyaya, Ideology and Perception*, Part V, *Concept of Rashtriya, op. cit.*, p. 25.
8. *Ibid.*, p. 26.
9. *Organiser*, 29 September 1962.
10. Bhishikar, C.P., *Pandit Deendayal Upadhyaya, Ideology and Perception*, Part V, *Concept of Rashtriya, op. cit.*, p. 168.
11. *Ibid.*, p. 174.
12. Golwalkar, M.S., *Deendayal Upadhyaya and D.B. Thengadi, Integral Approach, op. cit.*, p. 144.
13. *Ibid.*
14. Bhishikar, C.P., *Pandit Deendayal Upadhyaya, Ideology and Perception*, Part V, *Concept of Rashtriya, op. cit.*, p. 176.

6

JANA SANGH: THE POLITICAL PARTY

Jana Sangh was founded in 1951, four years after independence. Power was in the hands of the Congress. However, Congress had never been organised as a political party. It had all along been a movement. In a democracy it is necessary that any party must also have workers who accept the discipline of the party. The party prepares its programmes in accordance with its ideals and the workers are required to go to the people with that programme. According to Deendayal, "Although the Congress Party had styled itself as a party with certain ideals and had also drawn up a programme, yet it did not possess a suitable organisation and the required workers. Its style of functioning was to come together for contesting elections and, after winning power, to compete with one another in the distribution of that power and indulge in the game of power-politics. For a number of years, Congress continued to derive benefit from the credit earned for it by Gandhiji. Therefore, Nehru's popularity served as an asset for winning elections. The Congress Party never underwent an idealistic change. Persons from the market place can never become party workers. Hence Congress Party became an instrument for acquiring power. This was the beginning of its degeneration. In order to acquire power, it started to foment narrow loyalties based on caste, language, religion, region etc. It adopted the policy of appeasement of religious minorities. There were persons who became brokers of the vote-banks of these minorities. The government had lost contact with the people with the result that the democracy had now come to be understood as one party democracy. With this, the cult of personality also became the order of the day. People in the country started following individuals rather than principles. Congressmen well understood the importance of personality cult for acquiring power. It became a practice with them to please Nehru but continue in their evil ways. A new cult of holding political courts was started. The voters were reduced to the position of silent spectators for the intervening period of five years after every election. This was democracy in a degenerated form."[1]

Things had come to such a pass, mainly because there was no purposeful opposition party in the country. In a democracy, it is necessary for the common man to inculcate certain qualities. Otherwise, democracy does not succeed. The Indian society had not progressed in this respect, and consequently, politics became the means of serving personal and caste interests. He again asserted, "We failed to realise that for the success of democracy different qualities were required than those that had been developed during the freedom struggle. So, though democracy arrived, we failed to develop the requisite qualities to run it. No attempt was ever made by anyone to develop such qualities in our society. Character is important in social behaviour as it is in private behaviour. Honesty is as much social as a personal virtue. Politics, ultimately, is a form of social behaviour and for conducting politics, virtues like honesty and self-discipline are necessary. The Congress Party never tried to develop these virtues. On the contrary, it exploited the existing diversities and rivalries in the society to acquire power."[2]

Deendayal's Concept of the Party

Deendayal Upadhyaya had definite views about what a political party should be. He used to say, "Political parties of India today have several shortcomings. As a political party the standard of the Congress Party is the lowest. These days political parties are not organised with some fixed objective. They are formed on individual or group considerations. Idealism alone is of no use; idealism must be lined with national interest. The communists do have an ideal but that ideal strikes at the very root of democracy. A disciplined party and a dedicated and patriotic leadership are greatly needed today. A free press, independent judiciary, and a clean and efficient administration are the prerequisites of a successful democracy. In a democracy, there are bound to be more than one political parties but all parties must follow a code of conduct or *panchasheel.* Defections should not be encouraged. Then only can we have a stable administration in the country and see the end of irresponsible politics.[3]

Regarding the role of Jana Sangh, Deendayal had stated in 1956, "We have to bring about economic and social revolution in our country through peaceful means. But for this, the present 'family-leadership' is not useful; it is afraid of being dislodged from power in the event of such a revolution being successful and consequently, it has abandoned the path of the forward march of idealism. Moreover, all these leaders are of a particular age group. In fact, we are faced with a conflict between the old and new generation. To be frank, only such conflicts lead to progress. We are fully aware of the fact that the present day old leaders would never extend their support to revolution. The workers of Jana Sangh are anxious to create a new leadership. Jana Sangh wants to provide a new leadership to the country. But the old ways of creating leadership will have to be changed. The method of demonstrative politics will not be desirable for this. As such, we shall have to abandon all the wrong ways and adopt the correct path which will take us to our goal. Slogans, processions etc. are intoxicating. They cannot help in the emergence of new leadership. Let the leadership emerge on its own; it is no use to prop it up by artificial means.

"Therefore, for the success of democracy and also in the interest of our own party, we should keep the common man before us. The common man may appear to be a simpleton but in fact, he is quite intelligent. He is more valorous than the valiant. I want Jana Sangh to be a party of such common men."[4]

A New Field Altogether

In a sense, the attempt of Jana Sangh to organise the Bharatiya people on the basis of a democratic discipline and idealism in addition to party loyalty, was the first of its kind. The method adopted by Communists was to set up people's organisation by inciting public opinion and taking recourse to agitations. Their method consisted of harsh individual discipline, study, and social discontentment, instead of purity of individual conduct and a sense of social morality. The special feature of the Communist style of functioning was to intoxicate the people with the idea of revolution and to induce them to work and make sacrifices out of addiction to this opiate. Their expression of such intoxicated madness used to be through exciting language. This Communist style of functioning has acquired universal form.

The Communists do not insist on purity of conduct and purity of means. Gandhiji conducted a good number of *satyagraha* movements. Congress was, and still is, a party of power seekers. If a democratic administrative system is to be run for people's benefit, then a large number of such workers will be needed in the political field who are not corrupt and who are dedicated to public service. Deendayal himself was such a worker. He had acquired the experience of creating workers during his life in the RSS. Now he had to create such workers in the political field where qualities of gentlemanly and meritorious behaviour were at stake. During the freedom struggle, people were often filled with incitement for fighting with the enemy. Such a situation, which induces people to make sacrifices and to observe purity of conduct is also intoxicating. But in a democracy political workers have to first fight their internal enemies, e.g. sensual desires, anger, greed, temptation for popularity etc. Sant Tukaram aptly expressed this by saying, "Day and night, I am involved in a struggle going on within my mind and in the outside world".[5] This is a struggle which goes on all the time and never ceases. Deendayal had to create workers for Jana Sangh who would first fight these internal enemies.

Deendayal's conception of an ideal worker was that firstly he should possess the twin qualities of being able to function with malice towards none and should be a friend, teacher and well-wisher of the people. He used to say, "Let the national outlook of Jana Sangh spread all around so that our opponent of today becomes our voter tomorrow, our voter of tomorrow should be our member day after tomorrow and our member of day after tomorrow should become our active worker next day."[6] Another quality of an ideal worker was that he should have a feeling of affection for the down-trodden and a social commitment. Thirdly, the ideal worker was expected to work for a social change.

Deendayal was determined to create workers for Jana Sangh and build up its organisation on the basis of the threefold concept mentioned above.

Systematic Study

Like Samartha Ramdas, Deendayal believed in deep study of any subject undertaken and that a subject should be studied in all its aspects. Having been entrusted with the responsibility of drafting the constitution and the programme of Jana Sangh, he studied the constitutions and styles of functioning of various political parties of the world. While keeping in view his own concept of Jana Sangh, he also tried to incorporate the good features of other parties. The Congress method of collecting funds did not appeal to him. He decided to avoid it. The communist practice of organising Study Camps, however, did appeal to him. He also thought that the RSS practice of Guru Dakshina (offering to the precepter), based on spontaneous sacrifice by the common worker, was worth following. The practice of having Organising Secretaries also appealed to him and was adopted. This would ensure that organisational set up of the party remained unchanged in the event of a new president being elected. Like Gandhiji, Deendayal also insisted on participation by Harijans and women in organisational matters and got the relevant provision incorporated in the constitution of Jana Sangh.

Cadre-based Party

Deendayal was a leader who maintained personal contacts with thousands of party workers. His mind was always with the workers but his own thinking was ahead of them. It would not be wrong to describe him as a grassroots leader.

Deendayal was engaged in a grand experiment in setting up the party organisation. His main idea was that a worker should develop into a leader who keeps in constant touch with people and carries on a dialogue with them. He was instrumental in bringing prestige to the party. A detailed account of his work in this regard has been given by B.N. Jog in his book 'Politics for Nation's Sake' as following : "Deendayal had an independent mind and was quite independent in his thinking. Freedom was his internal energy which manifested itself in every step he took and in every word he spoke. Naturally, he always insisted that party policy, State policy or for that matter, National policy should not be formulated under any pressure. Indeed, his aim was to acquire power and to implement welfare schemes but for achieving this he did not want to create middlemen between the people and the administration machinery. Rather, he wanted to achieve this aim through workers who were committed to the people, to the party, to principles and to the nation. He could not conceive of people's welfare through the medium of bureaucracy. He wanted to build up a cadre of workers and change the face of the country with their help. He believed that Congress being in power was like Duryodhana being in power. He wanted to change the situation in the country with the help of workers and co-operation of the people. Party, politics and acquisition of power were merely the means of achieving that aim.

"Deendayal wanted the candidates for election and the party workers to be dedicated to public service. He wanted them to be disciplined party workers and work for the party with single-minded devotion. These days (and even in those days) the Congress worker has become broker for getting done people's work from the government. It appears that their guiding principle is to grab whatever they can and to distribute it between them and the bureaucracy on fifty-fifty basis. This is the feeling that is being created all around as a result of such conduct. Deendayal's conception of selfless worker was such that a worker should cleanse the cesspool of corruption. Collection of election fund in large sums leads to the prevalence of corruption from top to bottom. He insisted on election funds being collected only from such people who believed that Jana Sangh should achieve power and its aim, only by following the policies accepted by it."[7]

He further wrote, "While moulding workers he was very careful. He did not want workers to consider castes in their daily life. Not only this, he always insisted that candidates for elections should not be selected and constituency should not be allocated to them on caste considerations. His main insistence was on the qualifications of the candidate rather than on his caste and community, and on his being suitable in all respects. Once, while insisting on this, he had cited the example of Dr. Ram Manohar Lohia. Dr. Lohia was not selected as a candidate for a constituency in Uttar Pradesh simply because Dr. Lohia did not belong to the community which was in predominance in that constituency.

"However, Deendayal's workers were always mindful of their work and of the type of Bharat that they wanted to create in the future. He never let them go out of control. Those of his workers who were not used to such strict discipline would question him in many ways. To them he used to say, by way of advice, "Convert this anger of your into work. Take your restlessness to the people". He used to advance a number of arguments in support of this advice and would tell them by way of an example that, at one time, even Tilak had been accused by the British as 'creator of political unrest', but that accusation, in fact, proved to be the description of his virtue. After Tilak (fifty years after), Deendayal proved himself to be the creator of the unrest against Congress."[8]

Party—What it should be

Although Bharatiya Jana Sangh was politically inexperienced, yet it had a political vision. Deendayal not only gave a philosophy and set up its organisational structure as a political party, he also provided it with a conception about itself. He gave practical shape to these conceptions. Those days, M.N. Roy was expounding the philosophy of partyless politics. He wanted to introduce politics based on humanism. He used to say that he wanted the politics of power to be replaced by politics of freedom. He wanted to prove that politics could be practised without aspiring for power.

Such thinking was quite in order as an ideal dream. Deendayal's conception about the party was also, in a way, fanciful. Even so, it had an element of effort and achievement. "Which party is good ? A party is not merely a collection of people ; rather, it should be a group of people who are actuated not merely by the desire of acquiring power, but by the desire of achieving a specified goal. For the members of such parties, political power is not merely an end but a means of achieving its goals ; they are endowed with a strong sense of dedication. It is only this feeling which brings discipline. Discipline does not consist of mere observance of certain strict rules imposed from outside. Discipline can be lasting only when it is self-inspired, instead of being imposed from above. Discipline has the same place in the party which *Dharma* has in society. If there is a sense of dedication, devotion and discipline in the party, then there could be no groupism in it. Groupism starts only when personal interest is given predominance over party-interest. Groupism is a social manifestation of distorted and ego-centric tendency.A party becomes ineffective if it is beset with groupism. The third quality required in a party is that it should be set up for achieving specific objectives. The style of functioning and the policies of the party should be formulated in accordance with those objectives. Opportunism is not consistent with this. Insistence on commitment to the objective is the virtue of principled persons, not of opportunist and indiscreet people. Political parties and their leaders evolve life-values by their direct behaviour. The rules of social conduct emerge from such values. Their policies must be based on these values. Democracy does not merely mean the holding of elections. Democracy requires a well organised people. Only a well organised political party, working for some objectives, can create good political traditions."[9]

Two Wings of a Political Party

Deendayal had conceived Jana Sangh to be a disciplined, dedicated, and well-organised political party. He had said, "We have to show that Jana Sangh is different from parties. There is no dearth of parties in our country which give up principles for achieving power. We also, most certainly, aspire for power and shall achieve it without fail; but our aim is even beyond it. We shall never give up that aim."[10]

After Independence, political parties had formulated plans for development and used them in elections. The Congress Party drafted the Five Year Plan. The entire government machinery was harnessed for its implementation. In this way, politics acquired a new dimension of development. The Legislatures started passing laws in the interest of people. It was necessary to keep a close watch on these activities. As a result, workers elected as representatives of the people came to constitute a separate section in the political life of the country. However, all the workers of a party could not have become members of legislatures or Parliament; some workers are also needed to look after the party-organisation. As the legislatures and the Parliament functioned in collaboration with the government, they acquired a certain prestige in the government and the society. This, naturally, led to the generation of bitterness and rivalry within each party. The people's representatives got an upper hand. Since the Congress workers had forgotten that power was to be used for only public service, the party was divided into two factions. The prestige and honour, which came with power, filled them with arrogance. Deendayal had been careful from the beginning to ensure that such quarrels did not take place in Jana Sangh and to ensure that the workers did not lose sense of public service. A political party has two wings, consisting of legislators and constructive workers respectively. Workers of both kinds should have equal prestige. Both should work with the mission of public service. Deendayal wished both the types of workers to be complementary to each other. The constructive workers should perform the function of keeping the legislators posted with the problems of the society because they are in a position to maintain constant contact with the people and so they have first hand knowledge of the sorrows and sufferings of the people in the society. It should be the duty of the legislators to place these problems before the government and make efforts to get them solved. On the other hand, it was the duty of the constructive workers to take the policy and programme of the party to the people. Deendayal always made the two wings aware of their respective functions. As a result, Jana Sangh never lost sight of its objective of reconstruction.

Deendayal himself used to study many of the problems of the people. He also insisted on the workers and leaders of the party to undertake such studies. He used to assign to various members different subjects for study. For example, he entrusted the work of studying agriculture and farming to Nanaji Deshmukh. He also organised training camps for political workers. In these and other camps, the different ideologies prevalent in the country were also studied. On many occasions specialists were also invited to address the workers.

Deendayal laid stress on raising the qualitative standard of the workers. He always placed before the workers rules of conduct required to be observed by them. The first rule was for everyone to bear in mind that the interest of the country was above the interest of the party. The second rule was that workers should have a sense of commitment for the programmes and policies of the party rather than for individuals. Thirdly, even though objectives, principles and ideology are important for a political party, the secret of enduring success is the service of the people. The fourth rule required the workers to be devoted to the ideals. It was because Congress Party abandoned idealism that it fell a prey to opportunism and succumbed to temptation. Jana Sangh had not merely to dislodge the Congress Party from power, it also had to provide to the country a new ideal and a new political culture. The culture, which was known as Congress Culture, was eating at the roots of democracy. This culture was a perversion of democracy. He placed before the workers the goal of rebuilding culture. For achieving this, Deendayal offered many constructive suggestions and tried to create such models. He always insisted on politics being culture based. He used to guide the workers on these lines. Although Jana Sangh had several presidents, Deendayal was the only person who continued to guide the workers from 1951 to 1968 like a light house. He also insisted that there should be no personal animosity in politics; the leader of an opposition party should not indulge in spitting fire, causing harassment and opposing for the sake of opposition. He himself was soft spoken and wanted the workers also to be sweet of speech. He had personal relations with many leaders of opposite political ideologies including senior ones like Rajaji. Deendayal was firm in his belief and always insisted on what he believed. Even so, he was a gentleman and had a sweet disposition. He used to say, "Jana Sangh wants to properly present its belief. It, therefore, gives more importance to abiding relations than to immediate opposition."[11]

Multi-party Politics

Deendayal was of the view that Bharat will ultimately have a multi-party system. In democracy there should not only be more than one political party, but also parties propagating different ideologies; there should be a healthy competition among these parties. Defection should not be encouraged; however, a person should be free to leave a party if objectives of that party do not appeal to him. Those who defect out of lure of power do not do so in pursuit of any ideal. In view of all this, India should evolve its own independent political system. The British type of two party system would not be successful in our country. We should have a system which suits us. Only then it will be possible for us to give to our country a stable government and check the shameless race for power. It is for this reason that Deendayal insisted on there being a code of conduct for political parties. He was of the view that Congress should set an example of good conduct. But the Congress Party was incapable of setting such an example. The groups that had gone out of the Congress, as also some individuals, were setting up new political parties. Hence, it was the Congress Party and groups of ex-Congressmen who were looming on the political horizon of the country. Deendayal had suggested that political parties with well-defined objectives should conduct the political affairs of the country on moral lines. Similarly, he suggested that agitations organised for getting government policies changed, should also be in accordance with a code of conduct. As the government is committed to a political party ; its decisions benefit only that particular party. The opposition parties have always to take recourse to organise *dharmas* to ventilate the grievances of the people. As political parties organise agitations to highlight the grievance of the people, the government should pay immediate attention to such problems. It is indeed unfortunate for the country that recourse has to be taken to *satyagraha, gherao,* and hunger strike to get the problems solved during the period intervening two elections. The government's carelessness in regard to these grievances creates the impression that it bends only when it is confronted with *satyagraha.* In view of this, Deendayal had suggested that a way shall have to be found which is acceptable to all. It was wrong to come out with the threat to change the government on small issues. The major problems should be taken to the people at the time of elections, whereas the small problems should be dealt with on an all party basis by devising a mechanism for it.

"Political parties are categorised as being 'leftist' and 'rightist' because we think in Western ways. This categorisation does not convey a correct picture of the Bharatiya political scene. We proceed on the presumption that all parties can be classified into two such classes—leftist and rightist. According to this division, Congress becomes a leftist party as it has accepted socialism. But facts are different. Congress is helped by capitalists. On the other hand, Jana Sangh is considered a rightist party, because it has not adopted socialism as such. But its programmes and workers want to bring about far greater changes than the so-called radicals.

"Another way of classification will depend on wherefrom a party's idealism is imported. According to this, Congress, communists and socialists will fall in a single class, as all these are trying to implant foreign ideologies here. They do not consider the Bharatiya values and circumstances.

"Another categorisation is also possible. This consists of pro-changers and anti-changers. For example, Ram Rajya Parishad represents an ideology which is archaic and non-changeable. It is against all social and economic changes. As against this, Jana Sangh, like Swami Dayanand and Lokmanya Tilak, is desirous of bringing about social and economic changes while protecting our eternal values and ancient philosophy."[12]

Mass Contact and Propagation of Ideology

It was always held by Deendayal that Jana Sangh was not merely a party but a national movement. He wanted the Jana Sangh to have an identity of a party working for all round development of the nation and having an ideology based on Bharatiya culture. Jana Sangh was not a party established merely out of political expediency for achieving power. Hence, he wanted Jana Sangh to be recognised by the people not merely as a political party but as a national movement for basic change. For this reason, he always stressed that Jana Sangh should adopt the policy of setting up its maximum number of candidates to contest elections and try to secure, as many votes as possible. According to him, in this manner the Jana Sangh ideology could be presented before the people. Another method of propagating the ideology of Jana Sangh was to agitate on regional issues and he used to advise the workers to launch small agitations on people's problems. By this he aimed at mass contact and mass education.

Democracy within the Party

Deendayal's style of functioning was one of free and full discussion with workers. As such, in the meetings he would ask the workers to have their say and would listen to them. No doubt he placed forward his own views in these meetings. But he also listened to criticism. Several examples of this style of functioning can be cited. For example, even though he himself was a vegetarian, he was of the view that fish should be recognised as a supplementary food and that government should provide for the increased production of fish. In the same way, he opposed prohibition even though he himself did not consume liqour. He was of the view that the evil consequences of prohibition would far exceed the benefits therefrom. Even so, on such matters, he always encouraged the workers to express their views freely. In the same way he allowed free discussion on the concept of Integral Humanism.

Insistence on Basic Ideals

While Deendayal was soft-spoken and open minded as a party-organiser, he was very strict in his insistence on ideals. He often said that discipline cannot be imposed on a political party from above. A conduct conforming to the ideal was also part of party-discipline. It was very important for the workers to conduct themselves in accordance with the ideals of Jana Sangh. Here are two instances of how Deendayal insisted on principles and enforced discipline. In 1953 Jana Sangh had proposed abolition of Zamindari system without paying any compensation. Those days the jagirdars and zamindars were dominating the political scene in Rajasthan. Hence, five out of total eight Jana Sangh legislators in Rajasthan, favoured the zamindars and jagirdars and defied the stand taken by Jana Sangh on the abolition issue. Deendayal, without any hesitation, expelled those legislators from the party. In the second incident he compelled the then President of Jana Sangh, Maulichand Sharma, to leave the party, as it was suspected that he was collaborating with Nehruji and was about to reach a settlement with him. Ultimately, he did join Congress.[13] The workers had moved a resolution against him and forced him to quit the post of party president. Deendayal never tolerated any variance between principles and practice.

A New Direction to Labour Movement

The labour movement in the country was controlled by the communists, Congress and other leftist parties. If Jana Sangh was to make an impact on the country with its ideology, it was necessary for it to influence all the peasants, the workers, the students, and women. Deendayal was quite conscious of this need. For this purpose he held discussions with Dattopant Thengadi in 1955. Both had been inspired by Golwalkar. So, both had common views. In the discussion, some conclusions were reached. The first conclusion was that it was necessary to have a labour organisation which was not influenced by political parties, which was conscious of the real interests of workers and was rooted in national and cultural traditions of Bharat. Only then it would be possible to defeat the capitalist and the communist systems in a decisive manner. As such, Deendayal was of the view that the trade unions must be liberated from the influence of political parties and opportunism, and it was necessary to immediately organise such a labour organisation at the national level. In his discussion with Thengadi, he arrived at the following guidelines for setting up such an organisation:

1. The proposed labour organisation should rise above class considerations and should adopt a national outlook.
2. The labour movement should be liberated from or influence of anti-Bharatiya Capitalist and authoritarian elements.
3. The workers engaged in the labour movement should provide emotional leadership and should, at the same time be careful about protecting the basic interests of the labour movement. For example, there should be the right of association and a minimum living wage with proportional increase with rising prices. There should be security of services, workers should have the right of employment, of participation in management and of a share in the profits and should also have the right to strike if all other methods fail.
4. A sense of service and sacrifice together with a sense of responsibility towards the country and the industry should be inculcated among the workers.
5. All the trade unions should be joined together in a National Federation which should be kept free from all political influence.[14]

Women's Wing

Jana Sangh also organised its women's front for separately working for women. Deendayal was of the view that in politics women should be given importance like men. Their co-operation for building the nation should also be sought. It has been the tradition of Bharatiya women to work shoulder to shoulder with the head of the family. If those engaged in the political field did not pay attention to women, to their problems, and to their potentiality, it would amount to neglecting one half of our society. One cannot afford to show such neglect in the course of building a new Bharat. Hence, he paid attention to the setting up of a women's front in the Jana Sangh.

This women's front has taken a leading part not only in the constructive programmes but also in the agitational programmes of Jana Sangh.

Propaganda and Publicity

Jana Sangh laid stress on enlarging personal and regional relations. In view of the powerful propaganda of the Congress Party, every one doubted whether it would be possible for Jana Sangh to catch people's attention. But Jana Sangh was successful in spreading its wings all over the country with devotion, continuous hard work and through personal relations. It was successful in achieving quick political publicity under the leadership of Dr. Shyama Prasad Mookherji. Dr. Mookherji used to joke that Pandit Nehru was working as a good propagandist for Jana Sangh, for he was always making direct charges against the party, which automatically made Jana Sangh well-known. Some weekly journals like '*Organiser*' and some daily papers were also helpful in propagating Jana Sangh. When Jana Sangh members were elected to Lok Sabha it had the benefit of forceful speakers like Atal Behari Vajpayee who advocated the Jana Sangh point of view before the people. Deendayal himself used to write a political diary in the '*Organiser*'. This diary was, in a way, his ideological discourse to the workers and the people, and was useful in propagating the Jana Sangh ideology and its views on current issues. Processions were a speciality of Jana Sangh. The agitations on national and regional issues were also very useful propaganda. Jana Sangh fought elections in spite of unfavourable circumstances between 1952 to 1967 but established itself as a party with a distinct ideology.

In the very first election, Jana Sangh had secured 31 per cent votes all over the country. Hence it was recognised by the Election Commission as an All India Party. It must be accepted that the votes polled for Jana Sangh in the elections during subsequent 16 years were an indication of its increasing political influence. In all this propaganda and expansion, Deendayal's contribution was very large. The political circles in Delhi were conscious of the national thinking of Jana Sangh. Ideological influence does not depend on the number of votes alone. The novelty, the peculiarity and depth of thoughts are also important. Jana Sangh had not only earned political prestige as a representative of the nationalist point of view, it also came to be known as a stable pole in Bharatiya politics. This must be regarded as the fruit of Jana Sangh's propaganda and influence. The ideal of party organisation set up by Deendayal was not only an ideal for the Jana Sangh party but for entire Bharatiya politics. The guiding principle of Deendayal was that only a disciplined party could provide a disciplined administration.

REFERENCES

1. Kelkar, B.K., *Pandit Deendayal Upadhyaya, Ideology and Perception*, Part III, *Political Thought, op. cit.*, pp. 76-77.
2. *Ibid.*
3. *Organiser*, 27 February 1961.
4. Jana Sangh Special Issue, *Organiser*, 1966.
5. Kelkar, B.K., *Pandit Deendayal Upadhyaya, Ideology and Perception*, Part III, *Political Thought, op. cit.*, p. 30.
6. Jana Sangh, Special Issue, *Organiser*, 1956.
7. Jog, B.N., *Pandit Deendayal Upadhyaya, Ideology and Perception*, Part VI, *Politics for Nation's Sake, op. cit.*, pp. 125-140.
8. *Ibid.*
9. *Organiser*, 11 December 1961.
10. Speech in Vijyawada Conference, January 1965.
11. Kelkar, B.K., *Pandit Deendayal Upadhyaya, Ideology and Perception*, Part III, *Political Thought, op. cit.*, p. 86.
12. Jana Sangh, Special Issue, *Organiser*, 1956.
13. Andersen, Walter, K. and Shiridhar, D. Damle, *The Brotherhood in Saffron, The Rashtriya Swayamsevak Sangh and Hindu Revivalism, op. cit.*, pp. 160-64.
14. *Vivek*, 24 July, 1983.

7

ECONOMIC THOUGHT

According to the Bharatiya traditions, a nation is an organic living entity which has come into existence on its own and has not been made up of, or created by, any group of persons. A nation brings forth a variety of institutions to fulfil its needs, as well as to give concrete shape to its inner fundamental nature. The state is one of these institutions, which though being an important institution, is not supreme. In our literature wherever the duties of a king are mentioned, his importance is definitely recognised. This is so, perhaps, to make him realise his immense responsibility. He exercised tremendous influence on the lives and character of the people. Hence he had to give due attention to his own behaviour. Bhishma has said the same thing in *Mahabharata*, when he was asked whether circumstances make a king or a king makes the circumstances? He categorically stated that the king shapes the circumstances: *Raja Kalasya Karanam*. Now, some persons interpret this to mean that he considered the king above all. But this is not true. He did not suggest that the king was above *Dharma.* It is true that the king wielded a great deal of influence and that he was a protector of *Dharma* in society, but the king could not decide what constitutes *Dharma.* He only saw to it that people led their lives according to *Dharma.* In a way he was equivalent to the present-day executive.

In a modern state, the executive has the responsibility to execute the laws properly, but it does not enact laws. When the executive does not function with honesty and efficiency, the laws are entirely disregarded. One can well say today, "Executive is responsible for the present evils to a great extent." After all why has prohibition failed ? Who is responsible for the failure ? When those very persons, who have been entrusted with the task of implementing prohibition, start taking monthly pay-offs from the bootleggers, how will the prohibition policy succeed ? The executive is, therefore, responsible for the proper enforcement of law. This is the meaning of Bhishma's statement. It would be a mistake to interpret it as an acceptance of proved supremacy of a king. If this were so, how was it that the tyrant king Vena was removed by the *Rishis* and Prithu enthroned in his place? This action by the *Rishis* was never condemned by anyone in history. On the contrary, it was hailed by everyone. When the supremacy of *Dharma* is accepted as a principle, then, through the authority of *Dharma,* the Rishis derive a right to remove a king who defaults in his duty. Otherwise, it would have been absolutely illegal to remove a king from his throne. Thus, if a king does not act according to *Dharma,* it becomes the duty of everyone to remove him.[1]

In western countries, either a king was removed by some other king or people rejected the sovereignty of the king altogether. There king was a representative of God and could under no circumstances be removed at least in principle.

In our socio-political set up, the king and the state were never considered supreme. Not only that, there were other important institutions (besides the state, which was only one of them), to regulate and to help carry on the social life. Those institutions had been organised both on horizontal and vertical level, i.e. on regional and occupational basis. We have evolved *Panchayats* and *Janapada Sabhas*. The mightiest of the kings did not ever disturb the *Panchayats*. Similarly, there were associations on the basis of trade. These two were never disturbed by the state; on the contrary their autonomy was recognised. They devised their own rules and regulations in their fields. The *Panchayats* of different communities, *shrenis, nigams,* Village *Panchayats, Janapada Sabhas* and such other organisations used to frame their own rules and regulations. The function of the state was mostly to see that these rules were observed by the persons concerned. The state never interfered with the affairs of these associations. Thus the state was concerned only with some aspects of the life of the society.[2]

Similarly, in the economic field many institutions are created. We have to think what should be the nature of our economic structure. We must have such an economic system as helps in the development of our humane qualities or civilisation, and enables us to attain a still higher level of all-round perfection. We should have a system which does not overwhelm our humane quality, which does not make us slaves of its own grinding wheels. According to our concept, man attains Gold-like perfection as a result of development. Therefore, we have to devise such an economic system, to create such infrastructure and to frame such regulations in which and by which the inherent potentialities of man may find their highest fulfilment. Let us consider this point.

Economic system must achieve the production of all the basic things essential for the maintenance and development of people as well as the protection and development of the nation. Having satisfied the basic minimum requirements, the question naturally arises whether there should be more production for greater prosperity and happiness. The Western societies consider it most essential and even desirable to go on continuously and systematically increasing the desires and needs of man. There is no upper limit in this context. Normally, desire precedes the effort to produce the things desired. But now the position is reverse. People are induced to desire and use the things that have been and are being produced. Instead of producing to meet the demand, the search is on for markets for the goods already produced. If the demand does not exist, systematic efforts are made to create demand. This has become the chief characteristic of the Western economic system. Earlier, production followed the demand, now demand follows the production. Consider the use of tea, for example. Tea was not produced because people desired and wanted it. But tea was produced and we were induced to develop taste for tea. Now tea is a common man's drink. It has become a part of our life. Similar is the case with vegetable ghee. Did anyone ever want to use it ? It was first produced and then we were taught to use it. If whatever is manufactured is not consumed, there will be depression. Some of us may remember the Great Depression of 1930-32. There was abundance of goods at that time but there was no demand. Therefore, factories had to be closed down. Bankruptcy and unemployment were widespread. Thus now-a-days it is most important that what is being produced must be consumed.

The Editor of *Organiser,* an English Weekly, had gone to U.S.A. for a visit sometime ago. Upon his return he related an interesting instance.

There is a factory which produces "Potato-peelers", a device for peeling potatoes. The production of this factory outstripped the demand for the device. The management of the firm faced the problem of finding some way by which people might be induced to buy more potato peelers. They called a meeting of all the salesmen of the firm. Among the suggestions put forward, one was to make the colour of the handle similar to that of potato peel, so that along with the peel, the peeler may also be dumped in the garbage, often by mistake, Thus there may be greater demand. Also the product was offered in a more attractive packing. Now this economic structure is not merely consumption-oriented but is clearly leading to destruction. Throw away the old one, and buy a now one ! Rather than satisfying the need and demand of the people, to create fresh demand has become the aim of modern economics. Supposing that we need not worry about the limited supply of natural resources, there is yet the question of balance in Nature. There is a cyclic relationship in different parts of nature. If one of the three sticks, which stand with mutual support, is removed, the other two will automatically fall. The present economic system and system of production are fast disturbing this equilibrium of nature. As a result, on the one hand new products are manufactured for satisfying ever increasing desires, on the other hand new problems arise everyday, threatening the very existence of the entire humanity and civilisation.[3]

It is essential, therefore, to use up only that portion of the available natural resources which the, nature itself will be able to recoup easily. When the fruits are taken, the fruit tree is not injured; it may even be helpful to the tree. However, in the effort to take a greater harvest from the land, chemical fertilisers are used which in a few years' time will render the land altogether infertile. Lakhs of acres of land lie barren in America due to this factor. How long can this dance of destruction go on ?

The industrialist provides for a depreciation fund to replace the machines when worn out. Then how can we neglect the depreciation fund for nature ? From this point of view, it must be realised that the object of our economic system should be not to take an extravagant use but a well regulated use of available resources. The physical objects necessary for a purposeful, happy and progressive life must be obtained. The Almighty has provided that much. It will not be wise, however, to engage in a blind rat-race of consumption and production as if man is created for the sole purpose of consumption. Engine needs coal for its proper working, but it has not been produced merely to consume coal. On the contrary, it is only proper, always, to see that with the minimum coal consumption, maximum energy is produced. This is the economic view point. Keeping in view the aim of human life, we must endeavour to see how with the minimum of fuel, man proceeds to his goal with the maximum speed. Such a system alone can be called civilisation. This system will not think of merely a single aspect of human life but of all its aspects, including the ultimate aim. This system will be constructive rather than destructive. This system will not thrive on the exploitation of nature but will sustain nature and will in turn itself be nourished. Milking rather than exploitation should be our aim. The system should be such that over-flow from nature is used to sustain our lives.[4]

If such a human objective inspires the economic system then our thinking on the economic questions will undergo thorough transformation. In the Western economies, whether it is capitalist or socialist, value has the most important and central position. All economic theories centre around value. It may be that the analysis, of value is very important from the point of view of the economist but those social philosophies which are based entirely on value are far more incomplete, inhuman and to some extent unethical. Take for example, the slogan commonly heard now-a-days, "One must earn his bread". Normally communists use this slogan but even the capitalists are not fundamentally in disagreement with it. If there is any difference between them, it is only as regards who earns and how much. The capitalists consider capital and enterprise as important components of production and hence if they take a major share of profits, they think it is their due. On the other hand, communists believe only labour to be the main factor in production. Therefore, they concede major share of production to the labourers. Neither of these ideas is correct. Really speaking, our slogan should be that the one who earns will feed and every person will have enough to eat. The right to food is a birthright. The ability to earn is a result of education and training. In a society even those who do not earn must have food. The children and the old, the diseased and the invalids, all must be cared for by the society. Every society generally of mankind lies in the readiness to fulfil this responsibility. The economic system must provide for this task. Economics as a science does not account for this responsibility. A man works not for bread alone, but also to shoulder this responsibility. Otherwise those who have had their meals would no longer work.

Any economic system must provide for the minimum basic necessities of human life to everyone. Food, clothing and shelter constitute, broadly speaking, these basic necessities. Similarly, the society must enable the individual to carry out his obligations to the society by properly educating him. Lastly, in the event of an individual falling a prey to any disease, society must arrange for his treatment and maintenance. If a government provides these minimum requirements, then only it is a rule of *Dharma.* Otherwise, it is a rule of *Adharma.* Describing the King Dilip, Kalidas has said in Raghuvansha, "Being responsible for the maintenance, protection and education of his subjects, he was their true father. Their fathers were merely instrumental in giving them their birth. The description of King Bharat after whom our country has been named Bharat, also runs similarly, i.e. by maintaining and protecting his subjects, he was called Bharat."[5] This is his country Bharat. If in this country maintenance and protection are not guaranteed, then the name Bharat is meaningless.

Education—A Social Responsibility

To educate a child is in the interest of the society itself. By birth a child is an animal. He becomes a responsible member of the society only by education and culture. To charge fees for something which is in the interest of the society itself is rather odd. if due to their inability to pay the fees, children are left without education, will the society endure this situation for long ? We do not charge fees from trees for sowing the seed and caring for the sapling. On the contrary, we invest our money and efforts. We know that when the tree grows, we shall reap fruits. Education is a similar investment. An educated individual will indeed serve the society. On the other hand, it will not be surprising if people grow indifferent to the society which leaves them to fend for themselves. Before 1947, in all the princely states in India, no fees were charged for education. The highest education was free. In the *Gurukuls,* even food and lodging were arranged without any charge. The student used to go to the society for *Bhiksha. No* householder would refuse *Bhiksha* to the student. In other words, society used to bear the burden of education.

Similarly, it is rather surprising that one has to pay for his medical treatment. In fact medical treatment also should be free as it was in this country in the past. Now-a-days one has to pay even to get an entrance to a temple! There is a charge of twenty-five paise to enter the Balaji temple at Tirupati. However, there is a *Dharma darshan* at noon for one hour, during which period the payment of charges is not required. At other times it is as though *Adharma darshan,* when charges are to be paid. The society should guarantee to all its members minimum requirements for question arises if everyone is to be guaranteed the minimum necessities, where will the resources for all this come from?

Guarantee of Work

It is clear that the resources must be produced by our own efforts. Therefore, where a right to a guaranteed minimum is recognised, any individual who does not share in the efforts to produce is a burden to the society. Similarly, any system which obstructs the production activity of the people is self-destructive. Such a system will not enable the individuals to fulfil their responsibility. Not only that, but even if the requirements of an individual are met, while he does not share in the efforts, his personality will not develop fully, his progress as a human being will be distorted and lopsided. Man has stomach as well as hands. If he has no work for his hands, he will not get happiness, even if he gets food to satisfy his hunger. His progress will be obstructed. Just as a barren woman experiences emptiness in life and, consequent dissatisfaction, so does a man without work.

The guarantee of work to every able-bodied member of the society should be the aim of our economic system. Today we witness a very strange situation. On the one hand, a ten-year old child and seventy-year old man are toiling and on the other hand a youth of twenty-five is driven to suicide for want of work. We shall have to remove this mismanagement. God has given hands to every man but, hands by themselves have a limited capacity to produce. They need assistance of capital in the form of machines. Labour and capital bear the same relation to each other as that between man and nature. The world is a creation of these two. Neither of them can be neglected.[6]

Capital Formation

For capital formation, it is essential that a part of production be saved from immediate consumption and be used for further production in future. Thus capital can be formed only by restraint on consumption. This is the basis of capital formation to which Karl Marx refers to as "surplus value", in his treatise. In the capitalist system the industrialist creates capital with the help of this surplus value. In a socialist system, the state undertakes this task. In both the systems, the entire production is not distributed among the workers. If production is carried on through centralised large-scale industries, the sacrifice on the part of the worker in creating the capital is not given due recognition. The advantage in decentralisation is in the fact that the worker has a sense of direct participation in the management of this surplus value of capital. Machine is the most common form of capital. Machine was created in order to reduce the content of physical labour in production and to increase the productivity of the worker. Machine, therefore, is an assistant of the worker and not his competitor. However, where the human labour came to be considered as a commodity to be purchased with money, the machine became the competitor of the human being. The principal drawback of the capitalist viewpoint lies in the fact that by making the machine a competitor of human labour and thereby displacing and subjecting human being to privations, the very purpose of creating machine has been defeated.

Machine cannot be blamed for this. It is the fault of the economic and social system which cannot distinguish between the object and the instrument. It is only after considering the limitations of the machine that one has to decide upon its usefulness. From this point of view, to import the machinery from western countries, where shortage of manpower was the guiding factor in the design of machines, would be a serious mistake. The merits of machines are not independent of time and place. Machines are product of the modern science but not its representatives. Scientific knowledge is not a monopoly of any particular country. But its application has to take into account the particular condition of each country and its requirements. Our machines must not only be tailored for our specific economic needs, but also must at least, avoid conflict with our socio-political and cultural objectives.[7]

Professor M. Visweswarayya has said in one of his books that, while considering the system of production, one must take into account the seven 'Ms'. These are: man, material, money, management, motive power, market and machine. The skill and ability of the workers or those who should be provided with work must be considered. Easy availability of the required raw material, and the quality and properties of the raw material available cannot be ignored. We must also think of how much money is available as capital. How this capital can be increased and at what rate ? How best it can be utilised for maximum production ? How much of it should be put in the fixed assets and how much should be kept in the liquid form ? We must also pay attention to the form of power available in the country, in addition to the human and animal labour. Wind, water, steam, oil, gas, electricity and atomic power can supply the motive power. Of these, which form of power can be obtained, in what quantity and without being uneconomic, must be thought of while deciding upon our methods of production. In the same way managerial skills are also important and deserve due attention. If the ability to co-ordinate the efforts of a dozen workers is wanting, all of them will remain unemployed. It is also necessary to think of the usefulness of the goods produced in the society.[8] This means that production of any particular commodity cannot be justified economically without the consideration of the market it commands. Taking into consideration all these factors we should design suitable machines. Instead, we find nowadays that we install the machines first and try to co-ordinate all other factors afterwards. Other countries of the world did not progress in this fashion. Otherwise new machines would not have been invented. We are importing the machine and hence we have little knowledge. We shall have to develop a Bharatiya technology.

None of the seven factors is unchangeable. In fact, each one keeps constantly changing. Those who are entrusted with the task of planning must think of how the change is directed towards progress, how physical hardship is reduced, and waste of energy is minimised.[9] As an illustration, let us take the low productivity of our worker. It can be increased by using machines, and it is necessary to do so. But if the machine is such that requires only a few men to run it then the rest of the people will be thrown out of employment. If the machine has to be imported from other countries at such a heavy cost that the additional production it causes will be insufficient to make it economic, then such a machine is not suitable to our requirements. Just as to let a part of the installed capacity of a factory remain unutilised is a losing proposition, so also to let the people of this country remain unemployed is a losing proposition. Nay, this is even worse. Whereas a machine eats up only the capital invested in it in the past, the unemployed people have to be fed, which is continuous and unending drain on resources consumed at double the speed. No doubt *charkha* has to be replaced by machines but not necessarily automatic machines everywhere. Full employment must be a primary consideration and then the rest of the six factors suit this.[10]

Man's Place in the Economy

The use of manpower and the employment question will have to be thought of in the context of the human being as a whole, as an integral being. The economic theories of the past few centuries and the structure of society based on these theories are such that there has been a thorough devaluation of the human being. His personality is altogether irrelevant to the economic set up. Capitalist economy recognises only an "economic man", whose all decisions are based entirely on calculations of gain and loss, in terms of material wealth. For this economic man, five rupees are always more than four rupees. He works solely to gain more wealth, and exerts to get the maximum gain. For him, just like other commodities, human labour is a commodity to be bought and sold in the market.[11] This is free enterprise. It holds all other restrictions and regulations unjust save the brake of competition. In the race no one is prepared to stop and give a helping hand to the weak who is left behind; nay, elimination of the week is considered just and natural. He is uneconomical and, marginal, not fit to exist. This is what it advocates. By the elimination of such marginal units, the economic power accumulates in the hands of a few. This is considered normal and natural in a capitalist system. But when monopoly is established, even the check of competition ceases to operate. In such a situation the incentive resulting from competition is no longer available. Prices are arbitrarily fixed and quality of products deteriorates.

Even as regards the consumer's needs, the capitalist is guided not by the necessities and desires of the consumer, but by his purchasing power. The needs of the wealthy and the well-fed are attended to, rather than those of the poor and the hungry. As a result where countless varieties of goods are produced for the needs of the wealthy, even the basic necessities of life for the poor become scarce. The centralization and monopolization of production totally underline the influence of the consumer. The markets are so organized that the consumer has to go by standard products. This standardization is on the increase at such pace that individual preference of the consumer is ignored. Like the books in the library, even human beings are allotted numbers as consumers. The system which boasts of giving highest importance to the individual has ironically destroyed all individuality. Clearly, the capitalist system is incapable of helping the development of an integral human being.

Socialist System is a Reaction

Socialism arose as a reaction to capitalism! But even socialism failed to establish the importance of the human being. Socialists contented themselves by merely transferring the ownership of capital in the hands of the state. But the state is even more of an impersonal institution. All the business of the state is conducted by rigid rules and regulations. Generally, there is no place for individual discretion and even where such discretion is allowed, the slightest laxity in the sense of duty and social responsibility on the part of the administrators results in corruption and favouritism. The capitalistic system thought merely of the economic man, but left him free in other fields where he could exercise his individuality. The socialist system went much further, and thought only of the abstract man. After that, there was no scope for the development of the individual personality based on diverse tastes and abilities. The needs and preferences of individuals have as much importance in the socialist system as in a prison manual. There is no such thing as individual freedom in the socialist system.'

State's Claims on Individual

There is no private property in a socialist society. This removes the problems accompanying the institution of private property. However, the incentive for production and conservation of resources and economy in utilisation accompany the institution of private property. There has been no alternative arrangement to preserve these. The state is made supreme and the sole authority in all matters. Individual citizen is reduced to a mere cog in this giant wheel. There is no provision to inspire the individual to fulfil his role. As Milovan Djilas states, the class of old fashioned exploiters has been eliminated, but a new class of bureaucratic exploiters has come into existence.[12] Karl Marx put forward, in his analysis of history, that capitalism contains the seeds of its own destruction, and that communism is a natural and inevitable successor to capitalism. This concept may be helpful in fostering faith in the communists about their ultimate victory, but certainly such a determinist view destroys the urge for reform and dynamism in man. He is no longer the creator of a new order; he is merely incidental to a predetermined historical process. His task is only to accelerate the process. Therefore, even as he tries to organise workers, he cares little for their welfare, but uses them as mere tools for the revolution. The dialectic materialism of Marx, too, operates only so long as state is not established as supreme after destroying the capitalists. Thereafter the State puts a stop to the operation of the principle of dialectic materialism. In the name of crushing the counter-revolutionaries, the state becomes more and more totalitarian. The day when the state is to wither away, yielding place to a stateless society remains a mere dream. In fact, according to the Marxist view, to obstruct the process of thesis, anti-thesis and synthesis is itself reactionary. Marx is thus falsified by his own standards.

Both these systems, capitalist as well as communist, have failed to take account of the Integral man, his true and complete personality and his aspirations. One considers him a mere selfish being hankering after money, having only one law, the law of fierce competition, in essence the law of the jungle; whereas the other has viewed him as a feeble lifeless cog in the whole scheme of things, regulated by rigid rules, and incapable of any good unless directed. The centralisation of power, economic and political, is implied in both. Both, therefore, result in dehumanisation of man.

Man, the highest creation of God, is losing his own identity. We must re-establish him in his rightful position, bring him the realisation of his greatness, reawaken his abilities and encourage him to exert for attaining divine heights of his latent personality. This is possible only through a centralised economy.

We want neither capitalism nor socialism. We aim at the progress and happiness of "Man", the Integral Man.

The protagonists of the two systems fight, with 'Man' on the stake. Both of them do not understand Man, nor do they care for his interest.

Our Economic System

The objectives of our economy should be:

1. An assurance of minimum standard of living to every individual and preparedness for the defence of the nation.
2. Further increase above this minimum standard of living whereby the individual and the nation acquire the means to contribute to the world progress on the basis of their own *Chiti*.
3. To provide meaningful employment to every able bodied citizen, by which the above two objectives can be realised and to avoid waste and extravagance in utilising natural resources.
4. To develop machines suited to Bharatiya conditions (Bharatiya Technology), taking note of the availability and nature of the various factors of production (Seven Ms).
5. This system must help and not disregard the human being, the individual. It must protect the cultural and other values of life. This is a requirement which cannot be violated except at a risk of great peril.
6. The ownership—state, private or any other form—of various industries must be decided on a pragmatic and practical basis.[13]

These are a few general directions which we must bear in mind while developing our economy. *Swadeshi* and decentralisation are the two words which can briefly summarise the economic policy suitable for the present circumstances. Centralisation and monopolisation have been the order of the day for all these years, knowingly or unknowingly. The planners have become prisoners of a belief that only large-scale, centralised industry is economic and hence without worrying about its ill-effects, or knowingly but helplessly, they have continued in that direction. The same has been the fact of *Swadeshi.* The concept of *Swadeshi* is ridiculed as old-fashioned and reactionary. We proudly use foreign articles. We have grown over-dependent upon foreign aid in everything, from thinking, management, capital, methods of production, technology, etc., to even the standards and forms of consumption. This is not the road to progress and development. We shall forget our individuality this way and become virtual slaves once again. The positive content of *Swadeshi* should be used as the corner-stone for the reconstruction of our economy.

But one thing is clear that many old institutions will yield place to new ones. This will adversely affect those who have vested interests in the old institutions. Some others who are by nature averse to change will also suffer by efforts of reconstruction. But disease must be treated with medicine. Strength can be gained only from exercise and hard work. Therefore, we shall have to discard the *status quo* mentality and usher in a new era. Indeed our efforts of reconstruction need not be clouded by prejudice or disregard for all that is inherited from our past. On the other hand, there is no need to cling to past institutions and traditions which have outlived their utility.

The members of the Bharatiya Jana Sangh are not mere philosophers or academicians. We have set out with the determination to make this nation strong, happy and prosperous through the medium of the Bharatiya Jana Sangh. Therefore, we must carry on practical programmes for the national reconstruction on this foundation. We have taken due note of our ancient culture. But we are no archaeologists. We have no intention to become the custodians of a vast archaeological museum. Our goal is not merely to protect the culture but to revitalize it so as to make it dynamic and in tune with the times. We must ensure that our nation stands firm on this foundation and our society is enabled to live a healthy, progressive and purposeful life. We shall have to end a number of traditions and set in reforms which are helpful in the development of values and of national unity in our society. We shall remove those traditions which obstruct this process. Whereas one need not mourn the limitations of the human body, one must undergo the required surgical operation if any part of the body has cancerous growth. There is no need to amputate healthy limbs. If today the society is gripped with evils like untouchability which lead men to treat other human beings as lower than themselves and thereby threaten the national unity, we shall have to end such evils.

We shall be required to produce such institutions as will kindle the spirit of action in us, which will replace the self-centredness and selfishness by a desire to serve the nation, which will produce not only sympathy towards our brethren, but a sense of affection and oneness with them. Such institutions can truly reflect our *Chiti.*

Chiti is a nation's soul. The power that energises and activises the nation is called *Virat*, which in turn is aroused and organised and canalised by *Chiti*. The place of *Virat* in the life of nation is similar to that of Prana in the body. Just as *Prana* infuses strength in various organs of the body, refreshes the intellect, and keeps body and soul together, so also in a nation, with a strong *Virat* alone, can democracy succeed and the government be effective. Then the diversity of our nation does not prove an obstacle to our national unity. The differences of language, occupation, etc., are present everywhere. However, when the *Virat* is awake, diversity does not lead to conflict and people co-operate with one another like the various limbs of the human body or like the members of a family.

We have to undertake the task of awakening our nation's *Virat*. Let us start this task of awakening the *Virat* of the nation with a high sense of pride in our glorious past, a realistic assessment of the present and a great ambition for the future. We wish neither to make this country a shadow of some distant past nor an imitation of Russia or America.

With the support of Universal knowledge and our heritage, we shall create a Bharat which will excel all its past glories, and will enable every citizen in its fold to develop his manifold latent potentialities and to achieve, through a sense of unity with the entire creation, a state even higher than that of a complete human being. It is a state in which *Nar* (Man) becomes *Narayan* (God). This is the eternal and continuous divine form of our culture. This is our message to humanity at crossroad.[14]

REFERENCES

1. Golwalkar, M.S., *Deendayal Upadhyaya and D.B. Thengadi, Integral Approach, op. cit.*, pp. 55-56.

2. Ibid., p. 57.
3. *Organiser*, 13 April, 1964.
4. Kulkarni, Sharad Anant, *Pandit Deendayal Upadhyaya, Ideology and Perception*, Part IV, Integrated Economic Policy (New Delhi: Suruchi Prakashan), 1991, pp. 44-45.
5. Golwalkar, M.S., *Deendayal Upadhyaya and D.B. Thengadi, Integral Approach, op. cit.*, p. 61.
6. *Ibid.*, p. 62.
7. Kulkarni, Sharad Anant, *Pandit Deendayal Upadhyaya, Ideology and Perception*, Part IV, *Integrated Economic Policy, op. cit.*, pp. 82-85.
8. Visweswarayya, M., *Reconstructing India* (London: King), 1920, p. 26.
9. *Ibid.*
10. Golwalkar, M.S., *Deendayal Upadhyaya and D.B. Thengadi, Integral Approach, op. cit.*, p. 66.
11. Sharma, Jai Narain, *Alternative Economics* (New Delhi: Deep and Deep), 2003, p. 12.
12. Dijilas, Milovan, *New Class: An Analysis of the Communist System* (New York: Praeger), 1958.
13. Golwalkar, M.S., *Deendayal Upadhyaya and D.B. Thengadi, Integral Approach, op. cit.*, pp. 71-73.
14. *Ibid.*

BIBLIOGRAPHY

Aiyar, S.P. (ed.), *The Politics of Mass Violence in India* (Bombay: P.C. Manaktala & Sons), 1967.

Ambedkar, B.R., *Pakistan or The Partition of India* (Lahore: Mustafa Waheed), 1976.

Ambedkar, B.R., *What Congress and Gandhi Have Done to The Untouchables* (Bombay: Thacker & Co.), 1946.

Andersen, Walter K. and Shridhar D. Damle, Brotherhood in Saffron (New Delhi: Vistar), 1987.

Azad, Maulana Abul Kalam, *India Wins Freedom* (Madras: Orient Longman), 1989.

Baker, D.E.U., *Changing Political Leadership in an Indian Province: The Central Province and Berar, 1919-1939* (Delhi: Oxford University Press), 1979.

Bell, Charles, *Indian Mutiny* (London: Clarendon Press), 1931.

Bhambhri, C.P., *Bharatiya Janata Party: Periphery to Centre* (New Delhi: Shipra), 2001.

Bhishikar, C.P., *Deendayal Upadhyaya Ideology and Perception, Concept of the Rashtra* (New Delhi: Suruchi Prakashan), 1991.

Bhishikar, C.P., *Shri Guruji Pioneer of New Era* (Bangalore: Sahitya Sindu Prakashan), 1999.

Bimal Prasad (ed.), *A Revolutionary Quest* (Delhi: Oxford University Press), 1980.

Bose, S.K., *Tej Bahadur Sapru* (New Delhi: Publications Division, Ministry of Information and Broadcasting, Government of India), 1978.

Bose, Subhas Chandra, *The Indian Struggle* (Calcutta: Published for Netaji Publishing Society), 1948.

Chandra, Bipan, *Communalism in India* (New Delhi: Vani Educational Books), 1984.

Chandra, Bipan, *India's Struggle for Independence 1857-1947* (New Delhi: Viking), 1998.

Chandra, Bipan, *Nationalism and Colonialism in Modern India* (New Delhi: Orient Longman), 1979.

Chaudhary, Sukhbir, *Growth of Nationalism in India*, 2 Vols. (New Delhi: Trimurti Publications), 1973.

Chitkara, M.G., *Converts Do Not Make a Nation* (New Delhi: APH Publishing Company), 1998.

Chirol, Valentine, *The Indian Unrest* (New Delhi: Lights and Life Publications), 1979.

Chirol, Valentine, *India Old and New* (New Delhi: Lights and Life Publications), 1975.

Collins, Larry and Lapierre, Dominique, *Freedom at Midnight* (New Delhi: Vikas Publishing House), 1997.

Curran, J.A. Jr., *Militant Hinduism in Indian Politics: A Study of RSS* (New York: Institute of Public Relations), 1951.

Dalton, Dennis, *Indian Idea of Freedom* (New Delhi: Manhohar), 1982.

Das, Durga, *India From Curzon to Nehru* (London: Collins), 1959.

Das, Swaranmala, *Shri Aurobindo: A Political Thinker* (New Delhi: Ajanta), 1993.

Datta, V.N., *Madan Lal Dhingra and the Revolutionary Movement* (New Delhi: Vikas Publishing House), 1978.

Deodhar, V.N., *Deendayal Upadhyaya, Ideology and Perception, A Profile* (New Delhi: Suruchi Prakashan), 1991.

Desai, A.R., *Social Background of Indian Nationalism* (Bombay: Popular Prakashan), 1976.

Dharamvira, *Lala Hardayal and Revolutionary Movements of His Times* (New Delhi: Indian Book Company), 1970.

Dignon, Don, *The Indian Revolutionary Problem in British Diplomacy 1914-1919* (New Delhi: Allied Publishers), 1983.

Dwarkadas, Kanji, *India's Fight for Freedom: An Eye Witness Story, 1913-37* (Bombay: Popular Prakashan), 1960.

Gandhi, M.K., *An Autobiography or The Story of My Experiments With Truth* (Ahmedabad: Navajivan Publishing House), 1983.

Ghosh, Kalicharan, *The Roll of Honours: Ancedotes of Indian Martyrs* (Calcutta: Vidya Bharati), 1975.

Ghosh, Partha S., *BJP and the Evolution of Hindu Nationalism, From Pheriphery to Centre* (New Delhi: Manohar), 1999.

Golwalkar, M.S., *Bunch of Thought* (Bangalore: Jagaran Prakashan), 1980.

Golwalkar, M.S. and Others, *Integral Approach* (New Delhi: Suruchi Prakashan), 1991.

Gordan, A. Leonard, *Bengal: The Nationalist Movement, 1876-1940* (Delhi: Manohar), 1974.

Gooch, G. P., *Nationalism* (London: Longman), 1945.

Guha, A. C., *First Spark of Revolution* (Delhi: Orient Longman), 1972.

Gupta, Dipankar, *The Context of Identity: Sikh Identity* (Delhi: Oxford University Press), 1996.

Hardayal, *Hints for Self Culture* (Delhi: Rajkamal Publications), 1948.

Hasan, Mushirul, *Nationalism and Communal Politics in India 1916-1928* (New Delhi: Manohar), 1981.

Hasan, Mushirul, *Communal Pan-Islamic Trends in Colonial India 1916-1928* (New Delhi: Manohar), 1981.

Hingle, G.S., *Hindutva Re-awakened* (Delhi: Vikas), 1999.

Jhangiani, Motilal A., *Jana Sangh and Swatantra, A Profile of the Rightist Parties in India* (Bombay: Manaktalas), 1967.

Jog, B.N., *Deendayal Upadhyaya: Ideology and Perception, Politics for Nation's Sake* (New Delhi: Suruchi Prakashan), 1991.

Joshi, V.C., *Sri Aurobindo—An Interpretation* (New Delhi: Vikas Publishers), 1973.

Justice on Trial (Manglore: Sharda Press), 1968.

Kakar, Sudhir, *The Colour of Violence* (Delhi: Viking), 1995.

Karan Singh, *Prophet of Indian Nationalism* (Bombay: Bharatiya Vidya Bhawan), 1991.

Karnakaran, K. P. (ed.), *Modern Indian Political Thought* (New Delhi; Allied Publishers), 1962.

Keer, Dhananjay, *Veer Savarkar* (Bombay: Popular Prakashan), 1966.

Kelkar, B.K., *Deendayal Upadhyaya: Ideology and Perception, Political Thought* (New Delhi: Suruchi Prakashan), 1991.

Ker, James Compbell, *Political Trouble in India* (Calcutta: Superintendent, Government Printing), 1917.

Kothari, Rajani, *Politics in India* (Boston: Little Brown and Co.), 1970.

Kulkarni, *India and Pakistan* (New Delhi: Sterling), 1998.

Kulkarni, Sharad Anant, *Deendayal Upadhyaya: Ideology and Perception, Integral Economic Policy* (New Delhi: Suruchi Prakashan), 1991.

Malkani, K.R., *The RSS Story* (New Delhi: Sterling), 1984.

Masani, R.P., *Dadabhai Naoroji* (New Delhi: Publications Division, Ministry of Information and Broadcasting, Government of India), 1960.

Masselos, Jim, *Indian Nationalism: An History* (New Delhi: Sterling), 1985.

Mathur, L.P., *Indian Revolutionary Movement in USA* (Delhi: S. Chand), 1970.

Mazumdar, R.C., Roy Chaudhary, H. C. Dutta, Kali Kumar, *An Advanced History of India* (Madras: Macmillan), 1950.

Mazumdar, S.N., *In Search of a Revolutionary Ideology* (New Delhi: Peoples Publishing House), 1979.

McCarthy, Justin, *History of Our Times*, Vol. II (London: Chatts), 1897.

Mead, Henery, *The Sepoy Revolt: Its Causes & Consequences* (Delhi: Gyan), 1986.

Mehta, Ashok and Achut Patrwardhan, *The Communal Triangle in India* (Delhi: Oxford), 1942.

Mody, Homi, *Pherozeshah Mehta* (New Delhi: Publications Division, Ministry of Information and Broadcasting, Government of India), 1963.

Nanda, B.R., *Gandhi, Pan-Islamism, Imperialism and Nationalism in India* (Bombay: Oxford University Press), 1989.

Nath, Shaileshwar, *Terrorism in India* (New Delhi: National Publishing House), 1980.

Nehru, Jawaharlal, *An Autobiography* (London: The Bodley Head), 1958.

Nene, V.V., *Deendayal Upadhyaya: Ideology and Perception, Integral Humanism* (New Delhi: Suruchi Prakashan), 1991.

Nisbet, Robert A., *Community and Power* (Oxford: Oxford University Press), 1968.

Noorani, A.G., *Savarkar and Hindutva* (New Delhi: Left Word), 2002.

Parmanand, Bhai, *Hindu Sangathan* (Lahore: The Hindu Yuvak Sabha), 1936.

Parmanand, Bhai, *The Story of My Life* (New Delhi: S. Chand), 1982.

Parekh, Bhikhu, *Colonialism, Tradition and Reform* (Delhi: Sage Publications), 1999.

Pulkar, Narrain Hary, *Dr. K.B. Hedgewar* (Pune: Hari Vinayak Datya), 1964.

Purani, A.B., *The Life of Shri Aurobindo: A Source Book* (Pondicherry: Shri Aurbindo Ashram), 1964.

Radhakrishanan, S. (ed.), *Mahatma Gandhi* (London: George Allen), 1949.

Rai, Lala Lajpat, *The Story of My Life* (New Delhi: D.A.V. Publications), 1987.

Rai, Lala Lajpat, *Young India: An Interpretation and a History of the Nationalist Movement from Within* (New Delhi: Publications Division, Ministry of Information and Broadcasting, Government of India), 1968.

Rajendra Prasad, *An Autobiography* (Bombay: Asia Publishing House), 1957.

Raju, P.T., *Idealistic Thought in India* (Cambridge: Harvard University Press), 1953.

Ralhan, O.P. (ed.), *Hindu Mahasabha*, 2 Vols. (New Delhi: Anmol), 1997.

Rao, Ramesh N., Secular: *"Gods" Blame Hindu "Demons"—The Sangh Parivar Through the Mirror of Distortion* (New Delhi: Har-Anand), 2001.

Ray, Sibnarayan (ed.), *M.N. Roy, Philosopher and Revolutionary* (Delhi: Oxford University Press), 1987.

Reddy, P.L. Sanjeev and Mishra, S.N. (eds.), *Sardar Vallabhbhai Patel: The Nation Builder* (New Delhi: Indian Institute of Public Administration), 2004.

Rolland Romain, *The Life of Vivekananda and the Universal Gospel* (Calcutta: Advaita Ashrama), 1953.

Shankhdher, M.M., *Reflections on Indian Politics* (New Delhi: Kumar Brothers), 1973.

Sarojini, Naidu, *Speeches and Writings* (Madras: G. A. Natesan), 1945.

Savarkar, V.D., *Hindu-Pad-Padshahi* (Pune: Kelkar), 1925.

Savarkar, V.D., *Hindu Rashtra Darshan* (Bombay: Veer Savarkar Prakashan), 1984.

Savarkar, V.D., *Hindutva: Who is a Hindu?* (Bombay: Veer Savarkar Prakashan), 1969.

Savarkar, V.D., *Six Glorious Epics in Indian History* (New Delhi: Rajdhani Granthagar), 1970.

Savarkar, V.D., *Swantantryaveer Savarkar: A guide to Indian Revolutionary Movement* (Pune: Maharashtra Prantik Hindu Sabha), 1963.

Savarkar, V.D., *The Indian War of Independence 1847* (New Delhi: Phoenix), 1947.

Savarkar, V.D., *The Story of My Transportation of Life* (Bombay: Sadbhakti Publications), 1950.

Savarkar, S.S. & Joshi G.M., *Historic Statements: V.D. Savarkar* (Bombay: Popular Prakash), 1967.

Sehshadri, H.V. (ed.), *Dr. Hedgewar: The Epoch Maker* (Bangalore: Sahitya Sindu Prakashan), 2002.

Sehshadri, H.V. (ed.), R.S.S.: *A Vision in Action* (Bangalore: Sahitya Sindhu Prakashan), 2000.

Shankar, Ramahari, *Gandhi's Encounter With Indian Revolutionaries* (New Delhi: Siddharth Publications), 1996.

Sharma, Jai Narain, *Power, Politics & Corruption: A Gandhian Solution* (New Delhi: Deep and Deep), 2004.

Sharma, Malikarjuna, *Role of Revolutionaries in the Freedom Struggle* (Hyderabad: Marxist Study Forum), 1987.

Sharma, Rashmi (ed.), *Sonia* Versus *Vajpayee* (New Delhi: Deep and Deep), 2004.

Shraddhanand, Swami, *Inside Congress* (Bombay: Phoenix), 1946.

Singh, Gulab, *Under The Shadow of Gallows, A Story of a Revolutionary* (Delhi: Rup Chand), 1964.

Singhal, Jwala Prasad, *Sphinx Speaks: The Story of Pre-historic Nations* (New Delhi: Sadgya), 1963.

Sitaramayya, Pattabhi, *History of Indian National Congress* (Delhi: S. Chand & Co.), 1969.

Srivastava, Harindra, *Five Stormy Years: Savarkar in London* (New Delhi: Allied Publishers), 1983.

Suda, J.P., *Main Currents of Social and Political Thought in India,* Vol. III (Meerut: K. Nath & Co.), 1973.

Sullivan, O. Noel (ed.), *Terrorism, Ideology and Revolution* (Sussex: The Harvester Press), 1986.

Tara Chand, *History of Freedom Movement in India* (New Delhi: Publications Division, Ministry of Information and Broadcasting, Government of India), 1962.

The Collected Works of Mahatma Gandhi (New Delhi: Publications Division, Ministry of Information and Broadcasting, Government of India), 1968.

The Complete Works of Swami Vivekananda (Calcutta: Advaita Ashrama), 1994.

Thengadi, D.B., *Deendayal Upadhyaya, Ideology and Perception, An Inquest* (New Delhi: Suruchi Prakashan), 1991.

Trehan, Jyoti, *Veer Savarkar* (New Delhi: Deep and Deep), 1991.

Upadhyaya, Deendayal, *Political Diary* (New Delhi: Suruchi Prakashan), 1992.

Varma, V.P., *Modern Indian Political Thought* (Agra: Luxmi Narain Agarwal), 1961.

Vajpeyi, J.N., *The Extremist Movement in India* (Allahabad: Chug Publications), 1974.

Wardlow, Grant, *Political Terrorism Theory, Tactics and Counter Measures* (Cambridge: Cambridge University Press), 1982.

Walport, Stanley, *Jinnah of Pakistan* (New Delhi: Oxford University Press), 1965.

Walport, Stanley, *Tilak & Gokhale* (Bombay: University of California Press), 1962.

Wasti, Syed Razi, *Lord Minto and the Indian National Movement 1905 – 1910* (London: Oxford University Press), 1965.

Wedderburn, Williams, *Life History of A. O. Hume* (New Delhi: Pegasus), 1974.

Wilkinson, Paul, *Political Terrorism* (New York: Macmillan), 1976.

Zaidi, A.M. (ed.), *The Encyclopaedia of Indian National Congress* (New Delhi: S. Chand), 1979.

Zangwill, Israel, *Principles of Nationalities* (London: Heinemann), 1920.

Index